Ron Thom

The Shaping of an Architect

Ron Thom

The Shaping of an Architect

Douglas Shadbolt

with photographs
by John Flanders

Douglas & McIntyre
Vancouver/Toronto

Douglas & McIntyre Ltd.
1615 Venables Street
Vancouver, British Columbia
V5L 2H1

The publisher gratefully acknowledges the support of the Canada
Council, and of the British Columbia Ministry of Tourism, Small
Business and Culture for its publishing programs.

Canadian Cataloguing in Publication Data

Shadbolt, Douglas, 1925-
  Ron Thom

  Includes index.
  ISBN 1-55054-412-8

  1. Thom, Ron. 2. Architecture, Modern—20th century—
Canada. 3. Architects—Canada—Biography. I. Title.
NA749.T56S52 1995   720'.92   C95-910246-9

Editing by Brian Scrivener
Book design by George Vaitkunas
Printed and bound in Canada by D.W. Friesen & Sons Ltd.
Printed on acid-free paper ∞
Set in Scala and Scala Sans

Contents

Preface

I GOT TO KNOW Ron Thom in 1946 when he was in his final year at the Vancouver School of Art and thinking about building a house. I had just decided that architecture was my destiny and was about to leave Vancouver for the School of Architecture at McGill University (coincidentally, as it worked out, with Arthur Erickson). I had to return without graduating two years later, and Ron and I became very close friends as we both became apprentices to architects in Vancouver. After several years in close contact with him, I left to complete my university degree in architecture and to get work experience in the eastern United States and Canada. By that time my interests had become focussed on architectural education, and my career evolved in four architectural schools across Canada. During those twenty-seven years I travelled regularly across Canada and took every opportunity to visit Ron in Vancouver or Toronto and thus saw and discussed his work with him at whatever stage it was, met and came to know his friends and colleagues, as well as his wives and children from two marriages.

The idea for this book came as a result of that close relationship. On the occasion of his funeral in Toronto in 1986, at a private reception afterward for his close friends and his family, which took place in Massey College, I was struck by the range of interests represented by these people, and how much they revealed in their stories about Ron Thom's life and work. I was also struck by the emotional level of the discussion. A wave of affection and good-will was supplanting the genuine grief at his departure. As I knew few of these people, I realized that I really did not know the real Ron Thom, and that spiked my curiosity and started the sequence of events which has led to the production of this book.

Many, many interviews and two years later, I had found out more about Ron Thom than I was pre-pared to deal with, an uncomfortable situation at best, but one that projected me into a more biographical approach to his story than would otherwise have been the case. This has been further structured by my personal involvement with postwar Canadian architects and architecture, plus a longstanding teacher's interest in process more than product. These decisions were further fortified by yet another decision on my part to take a documentary approach to the photography of Thom's work.

My purpose in taking these approaches is to provide the reader with a number of word pictures of what is involved in the making of buildings, the client's and architect's role in the process, the influences that come to bear, as well as the ups and downs, the highs and the lows of that experience. These provide specific backdrops (dated from 1949 to 1986) in the postwar period against which to see and reflect upon Ron Thom's work and development as an architect on several projects under quite different conditions.

This project would not have been possible without the collaboration and generosity of Ron's family, partners, colleagues and friends. I have tried to acknowledge all of these people, many of whom have made substantial contributions to this book, in a long list in the back pages. However, I want to thank, particularly, a few people who have spent many hours with me to provide knowledge, encouragement, wisdom and first-hand information to help me formulate this text, to read it critically in its first crude stages and later to ensure the accuracy of some specific accounts and the more sensitive commentary. They are: Ron's wife, Molly Thom, my invaluable guide to and commentator on the Toronto years, people, projects and events; Dick Sai-Chew, who represented the interests of Ron's Toronto firm and suffered my recurring requests for details;

viii Ron's mentor and first partner, Ned Pratt, my former boss, friend, raconteur and passionate observer of the architectural scene in Vancouver; Paul Merrick, Ron's close friend and protégé; Doris Shadbolt, writer and critic, my mentor on this project, and her husband, my brother Jack, formerly Ron's teacher at the Vancouver School of Art, both Ron's friends and observers of his life and practise; James Craig, former journalist who gave one of the semi-final draft manuscripts a definitive working over to help me overcome a blockage; John Flanders, architect, photographer, both friend and sounding board; Brigitte Shim, Toronto architect and a Ron Thom fan, who got me going on this project; and my wife, Sidney, who has provided continuous support through the trials and tribulations of it, as well as valuable insights and commentary on Ron and his friends.

All of the effort would have been to no avail if funds were not available to cover travel and other expenses to visit all these people, and to document Thom's work.

This book was made possible by grants and assistance provided to me by the Massey Foundation and the Canada Council.

1 The Postwar Ambience

RON THOM was an architect of great talent and promise, who, by the mid-1960s, was recognized for his design achievements as one of the up-and-coming architects in Canada. He had entered the field of architecture at an opportune time.

The period between 1945 and 1970 was energized by a major economic expansion in the participating countries of the Second World War as their war production capacity was converted to peace time applications. In Canada the result was a major building boom. It began initially to meet the need for repair and replacement of worn-out or obsolete infrastructure. It grew with the need for an increase in the housing stock and related institutions created by the postwar "baby boom" and a fresh wave of immigration. As this population moved through elementary and secondary schools and universities in sequence, it created a demand for new facilities all along the way. Each step in this progression spawned still further building to provide for the expanding industrial, commercial and service sectors, so that a need developed for successive generations of factories, shopping centres, banks, office buildings, hospitals, clinics and so on.

A phenomenal expansion of knowledge in science and technology took place in this same period, resulting in a deluge of new information relating to all aspects of built form. Architects were faced with a situation in which new products, materials and techniques were available which required new skills or experience. The small number of craftsmen who survived both the Depression and the Second World War was totally inadequate to meet the needs of the building boom. Additionally, many traditional building forms were no longer relevant to the new social needs or aspirations. In this atmosphere many untried "visionary" ideas of the early modernists came up for review, re-interpretation and further development. Technical ingenuity and experimentation became both a necessity and a compulsion.

As in many other cultural activities in this period, Canadian architecture was strongly influenced in the late 1940s and 1950s by ideas emanating from the United States and Europe. On the architectural front, Walter Gropius and Marcel Breuer had arrived in the U.S. from Germany (more specifically, from the Bauhaus, probably the most important school of art and design in Europe at that time) via England and were ensconced at Harvard, heading what became one of the most influential architectural schools in North America. Gropius's successor at the Bauhaus, Mies van der Rohe, had also arrived from Germany to start a school of architecture and, in addition, to test and demonstrate his latest theories of architecture in the buildings for the new University of Illinois campus in Chicago. The complete works of the Swiss-French artist/architect Le Corbusier were published in sets in 1945. Frank Lloyd Wright founded Taliesen, his own apprenticeship-school in Wisconsin, still earlier. Richard Neutra and Rudolph Schindler were established in California. The projects and ideas of all these architects and planners and their disciples were the obsession of the postwar generation of architectural students. To varying degrees, they all influenced the quality and direction of architecture in Canada and the United States through the 1950s and 1960s.

Ron Thom, starting out, was immediately drawn to the work of Frank Lloyd Wright, Richard Neutra, Harwell Hamilton Harris, Rudolf Schindler, the Green Brothers and Bernard Maybeck, all in California, and, later, to the northwest coast architects Pietro Belluschi and John Yeon. All of these architects were dealing with the same problems of landscapes, materials and climate specific to their region. Coincidently, these areas had many similarities to various locations in British Columbia within reach of Vancouver. The work of these architects illustrated a great range of interpretation of modernist principles in their buildings, but particularly in their approach to the setting of a building in landscape. Thom, who was was searching for precedents and validation for his own experiments with projects in Vancouver and its environs, found these works inspirational.

While Thom and his colleagues (many of them graduates of the university schools of architecture), ardently dscussed these matters at work, the overall urgency in the architectural offices, certainly in Vancouver, was to complete whatever project was at hand in order to move on to the next one, which left little time for quiet reflection. Design decisions, for the most part, were made under high pressure.

A recommendation of the Royal Commission on National Development in the Arts, Letters and Sciences of 1951 "that the selection of architects for the design of all major government buildings [in Canada} should henceforth be the result of open, national design competitions" exacerbated the increasingly competitive atmosphere in the major architectural offices across Canada. The National Gallery of Canada Competition of 1952 was the first such competition, and it stimulated other public and private-sector sponsors to launch a series of national or international competitions over the next fifteen years. These included competitions for: the Queen Elizabeth Theatre in Vancouver; City Halls for Toronto, Winnipeg, Ottawa and Red Deer; the Fathers of Confederation complex in Charlottetown; single family house design (one sponsored by the Canadian Plywood Association, the other by Calvert Distilleries); the Smythe Road (Ottawa) Housing Competition (sponsored by Central Mortgage and Housing Corporation); art galleries in Saskatoon and Winnipeg, and the RCAF Memorial in Ottawa, among others.

The Massey Medal Awards, sponsored by the Toronto-based Massey Foundation, brought about a further eight successive national competitions of another kind between 1950 and 1970. They generated an acute competitive pressure that hastened the recognition and eventual independence of the most talented designers across the country, who were encouraged by their success to open or expand their own offices.

The Massey Medal Awards program also gives some indication of the volume of building in Canada completed in this period. Each competition drew 150 to 400 or more projects as entries, each representing one architectural firm's own pre-selection of one or two projects which it considered "its best work" completed over the previous three years. By the time the baby boom hit the universities in the mid-1960s, the Medal Awards had sorted out the strong contenders, and the new campus buildings became showcases for the best, and by then, maturing talent of this generation of architects.

There is no doubt that the Massey Medal Awards also had a powerful accelerating effect on the evolution of a national awareness of "Canadian" architecture, both by making an impact on the architectural community and by raising the consciousness of clients and the public through travelling exhibitions of the winning project presentations. Another important impetus was provided within Canada by several architectural journals at the height of this period, and by the emergence of a number of regional "home and garden" magazines with wide circulation. Publication of carefully selected photographs with minimal statements of design objectives, accompanied by descriptive paragraphs and commentary, led, by the mid-1960s, to a form of "star" rating and wide public awareness of architects such as John Parkin, Arthur Erickson, the Montreal group ARCOP, Eb Zeidler, John Andrews, Moshe Safdie, Cliff Wiens and Ron Thom, to name only a few. With this new status, these architects also came to know each other personally, through their invited appearances at conferences such as the series organized by the Alberta Association of Architects and held at the Banff School of Fine Arts, and as invited lecturers and critics at the schools of architecture in Canada and the United States.

This early phase of the postwar period was the time in which Ron Thom's career started and developed, and in which some of his best work was accomplished. It is also the period in which "modernist" ideals and principles were in the ascendency across Canada, but under close scrutiny and reinterpretation in consideration of their application to the different landscapes, climates and the national and regional social, political, and economic realities of this vast country and its emerging culture.

2 Growing Up

RONALD JAMES THOM was born on May 15, 1923, in Penticton, British Columbia, the first child and only son of a Canadian mother of Irish descent and a Scottish father.

His mother, Elena Myrtle Fennell, came from a Methodist Ontario family (her father was a farmer) in Kars, Ontario, where she spent her childhood. Like many other women in those circumstances before the turn of the century who had some ambition and an inkling that there was a more interesting life to be had beyond the farm boundaries, she became a school teacher for several years and then decided to seek higher education. She enrolled in Victoria College at the University of Toronto in 1907, graduating with a Bachelor of Arts degree in 1911. With that behind her she moved to Estevan, Saskatchewan, where she had a number of relatives. She soon found a job teaching, and decided to take up residence there. She had musical interests as well, and played both the piano and the organ in the local Methodist Church Sunday School.[1]

At the age of thirty-one, in 1915, Elena decided to take up Law as a career, so she moved to nearby Weyburn and articled to William J. Jolly. She completed articles and was enrolled as both a barrister and a solicitor on June 25, 1919, and continued her practice in the same office until October 1922. Elena Fennell was only the fourth woman to sign the Roll of the Law Society of Saskatchewan as a barrister and solicitor.[2]

Well-read, she had become interested in the politics of the day. During the eleven-year period she was in Estevan and Weyburn, the Methodist church to which she belonged was instrumental in the development of the radical social reform movements that led to the formation of the Co-operative Commonwealth Federation (the precursor of the New Democratic Party) in Saskatchewan, and its subsequent entry into Canadian politics in the mid-1930s.

According to historian Lynn McDonald, M.P.:

By 1914, the Methodists were the most progressive on the social programs, acknowledging the right of all people to adequate maintenance in spite of unemployment or seasonal employment. By 1918, the Methodist Church had condemned profiteering and all unearned wealth. It called for a democratic organization of industry, for labour to be co-partners with management. It also proposed a mixed economy based on substantial public ownership (natural resources, utilities, transportation and communications) and the establishment of controls over profits. The church's social goals included the raising of wages above a set minimum level and the establishment of a publicly funded old age pension. Committees within the church even recommended unemployment insurance, sickness and disability insurance, widow's pensions, and maternity benefits. At the extreme, the churches condemned capitalism in general as leading to war.[3]

Given Elena Fennell's background, it was not surprising that she became politicized and committed to some of these views, although not necessarily as an activist, and that, later, she would pass them onto her children in the course of their upbringing.

Ron Thom's father, James Anderson Thom, one of a family of nine children, was born in 1884. He was raised in Glasgow but dropped out of school at an early age in order to help support the family. By the time he was in his twenties he had worked in the coal mines, then had gone on to acquire some experience as a quantity surveyor and bookkeeper. Foreseeing little future for himself in Britain, in 1906 he joined the flow of Scottish immigrants to Canada seeking a new kind of life. James Thom was a resourceful man. Not trained in any particular trade, he was nevertheless willing to try anything, and found continuous employment. During the war,

Figure 1
Graduation photo of
Elena Fennell, 1907
(Ron Thom's mother).

Figure 2
Ron Thom, age 5

he went back to England to join the Royal Air Force in 1917, returning to Winnipeg in 1919.[4]

At some point soon thereafter, he decided he had seen enough snow and headed west. In 1920 he arrived in Weyburn and stopped there on his way to the Pacific coast. He was a quiet man, but he was very musical and loved to sing. His interests led him to the Methodist Church and its choir, and it was there that he met Elena. They became friends and, marrying in 1922, they decided to move still further west. They got as far as Penticton, where, as Elena had become pregnant, they stayed for a year. Ron was born on May 15, 1923. James had found a job working in a sheet metal shop and began learning that trade.

At the end of the year the family resumed its westerly quest, arriving in Vancouver in 1924. They liked it there and soon settled in. James found work that eventually led to the formation of his own business as a sheet metal contractor, and within the next few years he and Elena added two daughters, Heather and Mavis, to the family.

Thom's mother has been described by his friends as a bird-like, affectionate, very bright and determined woman, and his father as a quiet, tolerant, but shrewd man. They both kept up their musical interests and James sang in the Bach Choir. When Ron reached the age of five years, his parents decided that he should take piano lessons and found him a teacher. His mother was strict about practising, and fond of using the adage "always finish what you start." As a result, she kept him on a rigorous practice schedule, and as at that age he was keen to learn, Thom soon became proficient. Early photographs show him dressed neatly, complete with tie and shiny shoes. As he grew older, following the Toronto Royal Conservatory of Music's program, he entered competitions at their regional music festival in Vancouver and won prizes for his performance. His mother by that time had great hopes that he might pursue a career as a concert pianist, but other interests began to divert his enthusiasm.

By 1930 the Great Depression was underway. Vancouver, as the western terminus of the raiload across Canada, was one of the major arrival, gathering and departure points for men migrating across the country, desperately seeking work. Over the next few years the most visible signs of change were the increasing numbers of unemployed people seen at various locations throughout the city, often appearing at people's back doors asking for work at odd jobs in exchange for a meal. Elena was deeply touched by this evidence of the very conditions that the reforms of her church were designed to alleviate, and she became very vocal about the political situation and impatient about the progress of reform. In addition to lecturing her children on the necessity for education and hard work, saving and frugality, by her example she taught them to show generosity to others who were not as fortunate and who needed help. The Thom house was full of books, and, in addition, socialist tracts and pamphlets.

In his later years, Ron Thom recalled the frequent appearance of one or more of these unemployed people at the family dinner table in his youth. He was very proud of his mother's commitment and her ability to argue politics. While there is ample evidence of the influence of his mother's teachings in Ron's work ethic, his generosity and willingness to help old friends and colleagues as well by his drive to excel at everything he did, there is less evidence to suggest that her socialist leanings had much of an effect on him otherwise, or on his work. In his later life, Thom was only interested in the making of architecture. He reviled people who made an ostentatious show of wealth, yet he was as

comfortable working with wealthy people as with his other clients. He was naive and apolitical, and he railed at or shunned the problems of dealing with multilayered government, business politics or overly bureaucratic institutions

VANCOUVER AS A CITY in the decade of the Depression still presented many opportunities for an energetic, healthy young boy to explore at very little expense. Although shy, Ron Thom had friends whose enthusiasm for exploring what lay around them opened up new interests for him. Besides the usual games—baseball, lacrosse, football and so on organized at school—the proximity of Stanley Park or the mountains in North and West Vancouver (only a one-hour ride away by street-car and harbour ferry) offered hiking on miles of trails through the forests in the summer and cross-country skiing at the higher levels in the winter with parents and friends. The Thoms occasionally rented a rough cabin on the beach on Mayne or Saturna or another of the nearby Gulf Islands, and Elena would move there for a month in the summer with all three children. James would come over on the weekend. This early exposure to the spectacular landscape of the region in all its variety made a major impression on Thom, which became focussed in his art classes at junior high school by a fine teacher, Jessie Faunt. He had always loved to draw, and with her encouragement he started to put his energies into drawing and painting and began to lose interest in his music practice.

In his last year of high school, Thom discovered that he could complete his required courses in the mornings and enrol in the Vancouver School of Art in afternoon classes to complete his elective requirements. He sought his father's permission to quit music and enrol in the art school instead, and his father agreed. As a result, he did not complete his

3

4

Figure 3
Ron Thom (left) and Don Jarvis in downtown Vancouver.

Figure 4
Ron Thom (middle) and two other Art School students on a drawing assignment.

studies in music and did not sit for the final examinations to obtain a certificate, much to his mother's disappointment and, presumably, that of his piano teacher, Miss Faunt's sister, Edith. This was the beginning of his adolescence and first timid revolt against a somewhat over-controlled but affectionate and educational upbringing.

By the time Thom graduated from high school in 1941 at the age of eighteen he had tasted that freedom of spirit associated with a good art school, and he was set on becoming an artist. He had been turned into a high achiever by his mother's attention to his education and her constant pressure to work hard and to excel. Automatically, he began to build on his newly discovered talents and apply the same discipline, ambition, competitive drive and dedication to this new field.

The idyllic life of his early high school years was altered by the outbreak of the Second World War in 1939. One of the first signs of change was an increase in the opportunities for summer work. Following the Depression, the latter was a welcome change. However, the prospect of conscription into military service was in the offing. Despite that, Thom went directly into the Vancouver School of Art in the fall of 1941 on a full-time basis[5] and was able to complete the first year before he reached the age of twenty, the age when mandatory induction into the armed services applied. It was in his first-year course in Painting and Drawing that he met Bert Binning, who taught that course and who would become one of his most influential mentors.

Thom quickly developed a new circle of acquaintances. Among them were Christine Millard and Donald Jarvis, both of whom were taking the same course options. They became his closest friends at that time. The student life and the ambience of the Art School were exactly what Thom needed to open

Figure 5
Ron Thom, age 23. Drawing
by Don Jarvis.

up his adolescent world. By the end of the year, he and Chris were in love and inseparable, but his free time had run out.

Both Thom and Jarvis signed up with the Royal Canadian Air Force in 1942.[6] Thom had wanted to become a pilot but, because of some technicality, was enrolled instead in the aero engine mechanic's course in order to be able to become a flight engineer/navigator. He was immediately posted to and moved around various coastal bases, all near Vancouver. The following year he and Chris were married while he was on leave. In mid-1943 he was posted to Alaska as a result of the RCAF's ground-support commitments to joint Canadian and American coastal patrol activities. At one point he found himself on an American base in a remote settlement called Umnak, in the Aleutian Island chain. (He told his sister, Mavis, that "he was so far west he could hear the Japanese starting their engines in the mornings.") That posting only lasted four months, and he was again shunted from one coastal station to another, and subsequently sent to the prairies for aircrew training as a flight engineer and navigator. The war was over within four days of his completion of this course and his promotion to Technical Sergeant, so that he was able to return to Vancouver unscathed for demobilization in time to re-enrol in the VSA in September 1945.

The second and third years leading to graduation from the VSA proved to be the most formative educational experience of Ron Thom's life, as it defined his long-term career direction.

3 Finding a Focus

WHEN HE RETURNED to the VSA after the war, Thom was fortunate to come under the influence of three remarkable teachers: Bert Binning, Fred Amess and Jack Shadbolt. Of them, Binning was the most influential because of his personal interest in architecture, particularly the integration of art and architecture.[1]

Binning had designed his own house and had it built on a beautiful site in West Vancouver. It was one of the first modernist flat-roof houses built in this area—which in itself was something of a breakthrough, since the mortgage company had to be convinced of the marketability of this "unconventional" form, hence it paved the way for others later. The significance of the flat roof as a building form lies in the potential liberation it gives to the plan shape and section, yielding a great freedom to adapt a house to sloping and unusual sites, and allowing the admission of light between the roof planes into otherwise deep interior spaces. By this means, Binning provided an interior gallery for his own paintings. When the house was complete, he painted a large mural on the exterior entrance wall. Considering other houses built in Vancouver in 1942, this was a radical and pioneering project.

While Binning's painting had been influenced by his exposure to the Purists in Europe, his own love of the West Coast environment and his great sense of humour combined to give his new paintings a recognizable, even if abstract, but whimsical regionalism. Similarly, his house was as influenced by his long association with small boats as it was by anything he may have learned from an exposure to Ozenfant and Le Corbusier's work. Aside from the white ceilings and some white walls, the remaining walls were all west coast cedar. The wide door-trim boards were finished with high-gloss white enamel and outlined with varnished B.C. fir. What he accomplished was to define a regional vocabulary which was imitated immediately and labelled, in Vancouver at least, the "West Coast Style."

By this demonstration, Binning had little difficulty persuading the Director of the VSA, Charles Scott, to allow him to introduce a short course on architectural design. The course consisted of having students study house plans in books and architectural magazines, then discuss the principles of their planning and design. Binning encouraged his students to experiment with models in order to understand simple structures, and to design furniture, kitchens and houses. Thus he opened yet another field of interest to Ron Thom, who was enrolled in the course, at a particularly formative time.

Another teacher in the School, Fred Amess, had started "The Art in Living Group," composed of a collection of VSA students and graduates interested in what kind of building environments they would be living in in the postwar world. Under the guidance of Amess and Binning this was to become an activist group with a mission. Many of the students had taken Binning's drawing course and had their interest in architecture sharpened, the more serious among them toying with the idea of building their own houses. As a group, they began, according to Scott Watson, to *learn about modern architecture from books, where the pictures of buildings, always taken under flattering conditions, illustrated the inspiring utopian ideals of the modern movement. Sensing that an economic boom would follow the war, the artists, led by Amess and Binning, planned a massive intervention in architecture and planning. They were convinced of the central belief of the modern movement—simply, that good design had an uplifting moral and spiritual effect.*[2]

The group developed a series of four public exhibitions to raise awareness and to start people thinking about alternatives to current living environments.

These focussed on examples of modernist buildings and their interiors, on the planning of single houses, residential communities and schools to illustrate possibilities and examples of more satisfactory forms for parts of the living enviroment.

Because of this activity at the art school, Binning became involved with still another group of students from the University of British Columbia and Vancouver architectural offices who wanted to get a university program in architecture started. In 1946, building on these combined interests, he persuaded the university and some businessmen to sponsor a week-long visit in Vancouver of Richard Neutra, a European-trained modernist architect living in California. This event was highly successful in every way. The art school students got close exposure to one of the most important protagonists of the ideas they themselves were espousing, and the university students and their sponsors got their School of Architecture.

IN THE TWO YEARS after the war when he was in the Art School as a full-time student, Thom was able to spend only a portion of his day working on the architectural projects devised by Binning and Amess for these minor courses, since he had other commitments. At that stage he was showing evidence of becoming a serious painter under another demanding teacher, Jack Shadbolt. What he had discovered, however, was that he had a natural capacity for three-dimensional visualization, and he was able to read, interpret and produce architectural designs and drawings as if he had been doing them all his life.

Thom was an intense and highly motivated student showing early the traits of the "workaholic." Using all the time available after completing his assignments, he studied the work of Neutra and Frank Lloyd Wright. He was soon drawing versions of "Usonian" houses (a type of family house Wright had proposed as part of his design for a utopian city) and trying to adapt them into something he could build himself. He said, much later, *Binning taught me to see, and he taught me to think. He was one of the most important teachers in my life. The strongest thing he taught us, which has had a profound influence on everything I've done in architecture since, was that every aspect of the design had to respond directly to the world around it, whether it be colour or form, or where the light came in, or the views looking out.*[3]

Thom clearly had the priorities of an architect regarding what was important in the design of a building.

I MET RON THOM by coincidence at about this time. I had managed to talk myself into a job in the office of Ned Pratt, an architect in Vancouver, as his personal draftsman for one year which lasted until August 1947, when I left (at the persuasion of friends on his staff) to go to the School of Architecture at McGill University. On my return in the summer of 1949 I was put to work temporarily in one of the firm's branch offices next to an old friend, Dave Hickman. Ned came in one afternoon with a drawing problem. He was in the design process on a very large and complicated house on a difficult waterfront site in West Vancouver, and he needed some coloured perspective renderings to show his clients. They were beyond my capability, and that of the others in that office. I suggested he call my brother, Jack, at the Vancouver School of Art to see if he had anyone who could do it. Ron Thom showed up with Don Jarvis, and Ned decided to give them a chance to demonstrate what they could do.

Ron was back in a couple of days and pinned up a watercolour rendering that stunned us all. It was on a 24"x30" sheet of 300 lb. heavily textured

Figure 6
B.C. Binning house, designed
by Bert Binning, in collaboration with Ned Pratt, whose firm
provided technical assistance
and supervised its construction.
It was built in the mid-1940s,
and is one of the first modern
houses built in Vancouver. The
trellis in this form is a recent
addition.

Whatman's watercolour paper. The view was taken as if from a boat out in the bay looking back to the house against the cliffs. The house was drawn in detail, but its size on that board was only about 3" square. The whole of the rendering was a superb watercolour painting of the fall landscape of the cliff, the trees, the beach and the water, but you could hardly see the house. A beautiful picture, but not quite what Ned had in mind! For me, this incident was the start of a long-term friendship with Ron.

THOM, AT THE AGE OF 24, and Chris had graduated from the VSA in 1947. Their contemporaries included a good number of strong landscape painters, and Jack Shadbolt had encouraged them to start exhibiting as a group. In addition to the Thoms, these included Bruce and Joan Boyd, Don Jarvis and Jim MacDonald. All of them had started families or were intent on starting one, and so had been talking about buying lots next to each other and building houses together. They had located a street in North Vancouver where the lots were available, suitable and affordable—(cost:$60 per lot / taxes $6 per year).4 Ron and Chris were the only ones who followed through and purchased a lot. They were joined by two former war-artists, Molly and Bruno Bobak, who took an adjacent lot.

Thom and Jarvis continued to freelance as commercial artists off and on for one year during which Thom started building his house. Time was running out for him. Chris was pregnant with their first son, Robin, in 1949, and the matter of a liveable income and an unfinished house urgently required his full attention. It was then he decided that, above all, he wanted to be an architect, but only if he could learn while employed. His art school education had used up his veteran's allowance and he had no money with which to go to university. Binning, who was by

this time teaching in the School of Architecture at UBC, saw also that the war vet students at the School needed a lot of help with drawing, and he persuaded the director, Fred Lasserre, to hire Thom to assist him with this task. He also involved Thom in some of the 'design crits'—the critical analysis of student design projects in a semi-public verbal exchange—thus giving him a first taste of architectural education at the university. The experience was useful, but Thom's overall financial problems eliminated any consideration that further education might be possible for him at this time. Building his own house had top priority, but it was only while doing it that he learned that there was an official way he could achieve his goal, by a period of paid apprenticeship to a registered architect and then completing examinations for registration as an architect.

4   The Firm

THESE DAYS, the normal route to registration as an architect in British Columbia involves a two-stage process based on a five-year university program leading to a professional degree, or equivalent, plus a minimum period of three years of monitored office experience, terminating upon successful completion of registration examinations. In 1949, when Ron Thom entered the field in Vancouver, the requirements were considerably simpler, and he chose a route no longer available, that of the apprentice. The process involved signing "articles" (a legal agreement) to work for one employer for a four-year period, while, as a spare-time activity, studying for, writing and passing examinations set by the Architectural Institute of British Columbia. The employer undertook to train the apprentice to become an architect, but there was no agreed timetable, time limit or course of study, nor was there any obligation to pay him or her. Indeed, in some cases, the apprentice paid for the privilege. Most architects who agreed to take on apprentices put them on salary as soon as they became useful. The articles were renewable for additional four-year periods, and they were transferable, but not easily.

Thom was encouraged by Bert Binning and others to approach Ned Pratt, a partner in the fastest-growing office in Vancouver, to see if he would take him on. Pratt had attended one of Binning's crits and, recognizing Thom from that early attempt at rendering a perspective drawing, was impressed with Thom's development and perspicacity as a critic, considering his lack of formal education in architecture. Thom's opportunity came in due course, and after giving him a short cross-examination, Pratt agreed to take him on. Thom was indentured to the firm of Sharp and Thompson, Berwick, Pratt effective June 1, 1949, with Pratt as his mentor. For the next twenty-one years, the firm provided the focus for his development as an architect, and Ned Pratt became successively his role-model and bête-noir. Thom had been well-advised in his choice of firm, as it quickly became the leading and largest firm in Vancouver in those years he was associated with it.

TWO ENGLISH ARCHITECTS, Thornton Sharp and Charles Thompson, emigrated to Canada at the turn of the century and set up their own firm in Vancouver in 1908, soon becoming highly regarded and successful. In the early 1920s, they won the commission to design and build the new University of British Columbia in a design competition to select a Master Plan, but were able to build only two permanent buildings (the Science laboratory building and the centre section of the Library) and a number of temporary buildings before the Depression set in. With these and other commissions, they were, however, more successful than most of the other Vancouver architects during this period. The university project came alive again in 1945 and provided the impetus to the early postwar development of the office, giving it a headstart in what became a highly competitive building climate.

Ned Pratt first came to Mr. Thompson's attention when his daughter brought him home to play tennis. Pratt, nineteen and a student at UBC, was an instant hit: a natural athlete on the rowing team grooming for the 1933 Olympic Games, well educated and with the manners of a gentleman. Thompson and Pratt became good friends, and with his elder's encouragement, Pratt started to take an interest in architecture. On his return from the Games he decided to go to the School of Architecture at the University of Toronto with Bob Berwick, who was working in the Sharp and Thompson office for the summer. They returned each summer, and when they graduated in 1938,

ARTICLES OF STUDENTSHIP

THIS INDENTURE made this 1st of June, A.D. 1949

BETWEEN
RONALD J. THOM,
in the City Of North Vancouver
in the Province of British Columbia,
student,
OF THE FIRST PART

and SHARP & THOMPSON, BERWICK, PRATT,
of 626 West Pender Street in the City of Vancouver,
in the Province of British Columbia, Architects,
OF THE SECOND PART

WITNESSETH that the said student of his own free will hath placed and bound himself, and by those present doth place and bind himself to the Architect, to serve from the day of the date hereof for a term of four (4) years.

AND the said student shall and will, faithfully, and diligently serve the said Architect as his student in the practise of the profession of an Architect from the date hereof, and diligently attend the business and concerns of the said Architect from the date hereof, during and until the full end of the herein before mentioned term, and that he will in all respects acquit and demean himself as an honest, faithful and diligent student and as an apprentice ought to do, and will obey all lawful and reasonable commands of the said Architect, and will not depart or absent himself from the service of the said Architect at any time during the said term without his consent first obtained.

IN CONSIDERATION WHEREOF the said Architect hereby covenants with the said Student that he will accept and take him as his student, and also that he, the said Student will, during the said term, and provided he shall continue to practise as an Architect, instruct the student according to the best of his facilities, power, skill and knowledge, or cause him to be so instructed in the profession of an Architect and in all things incidental thereto in such a manner as he now practises or may at any time hereinafter during the said term practise the same.

Nothing herein contained shall oblige the Architect to remunerate or maintain the said student.

If the said Architect agrees then it shall be lawful for the said student upon two (2) months notice in writing to terminate the said term and his obligations hereunder and in such event the Architect shall be freed from any further obligation hereunder and will, at the request of the said student, assign these articles.

IN WITNESS THEREOF the said student and Architect have hereunto set their hands and seals the day and year first above written.

SIGNED SEALED AND DELIVERED
in the presence of:

| _____ | _____ | _____ |
| Mona G. Hickman, witness | Charles Edward Pratt | Ronald James Thom |

(copied from the original document in the Archive, Architectural Institute of British Columbia, with permission)

both were taken on on a full-time basis. Born in Boston but raised in Victoria and Vancouver, Pratt became a naturalized Canadian when war broke out the following year. Both he and Berwick joined the RCAF in 1941, and both became Works officers on isolated B.C. coastal aircraft stations for the next four years.

When the war was over, Mr. Sharp decided to retire, and phase-out conditions were agreed between the partners. Mr. Thompson then offered Berwick and Pratt partnerships, which they eagerly accepted, and the firm was renamed "Thompson, Berwick, Pratt, Architects." There was, of course, the expectation that each of them would develop his own clientele, and they set about it immediately. The firm had built a lot of houses during the Depression,[1] and in the process, it had built with a wide circle of influential people a close relationship which led to larger projects. Berwick and Pratt were immediately successful in their attempts to follow this example with their war-time friends, and the results reflect both their different backgrounds and their winning personalities, as well as the postwar building boom. Most of these house clients went on to become influential business persons and Berwick and Pratt's clients for a wide range of later projects.

Not only was the need for new facilities of all kinds inevitable, but once started, the demand could not be turned off. The variables in the buildings as built are attributable to the changing levels of affluence of the postwar generation as it moved into the workforce with a higher level of education, optimistic expectations and entirely new opportunities arising from the knowledge revolution occurring in the same period, particularly in business, science and technology. The first twenty-five years of this boom provided a bonanza for architects, who, at the time, were in short supply. There was so much work that Thom and many others who started in the late 1940s thought they would always be able to pick-and-choose from a diverse and endless stream of projects, and "the better you were the more choice you would have." Precedents were there: Bob Berwick, on one trip up the Fraser Valley in the 1950s, came back with contracts for thirty schools! The firm built more than two hundred schools before the end of the next decade. Jessiman and Hickman's team in their office at UBC completed twenty-eight university buildings in two years (1958-59).[2] The vision of a constantly productive future seemed a given.

Pratt had few contacts at first, but he had a very clear focus and strategy. In an interview, he told me he had little interest in work outside the Vancouver area so he deliberately set out to make himself and his work as different as possible from any other architect and his work in Vancouver. He was particularly contemptuous of some of the few remaining old-time architects whom he regarded as "prostitutes at the beck-and-call of their clients." He resolved to take a stand for "contemporary architecture" and to be prepared to tell a client to "get someone else if he didn't like what he was proposing."[3] He adopted the credo that "form follows function" and tried to demonstrate this in his own work. His first new projects were mostly houses, and he chose to design them to be uncompromisingly modern, simple and open in their planning, using post-and-beam construction. Additionally, he made himself conspicuous. He cultivated a shell of roughness. He played hard and otherwise sought to attract the attention of the rising generation of potential clients.

Despite his advocacy of an extreme modernist approach in design, Pratt was at heart a Romantic in

Figure 7
Ned Pratt, a 1962 caricature
and accurate likeness drawn by
Barry Downs on the occasion of
the Royal Architectural Institute
of Canada's Annual Assembly,
that year in Vancouver, when
Pratt was President of the
Architectural Institute of B.C.

taste and style, given to the use of explicit visual and visceral verbal images and lusty humour drawn from a wide reading background of historical and Romantic literature. All of this worked very successfully for him as a way of establishing a presence or position in the eyes of the client world made up of his contemporaries. It also made him a popular and powerful role model for Thom and others in that office.

As the combined volume of work started to come in, Pratt and his partners soon found that they had to delegate all of the developmental part of it to others, and most of the design stage as well. Pratt had become a good analyst and critic able to get directly to the heart of the problem at the conceptual stage, which gave him credibility with an increasingly sophisticated and ambitious staff, most of whom were graduates of the postwar schools of architecture who were committed to modernist ideas. He was thus able to develop and maintain the leadership role in the office as the arbiter of design quality on all the major non-institutional projects. He also became a talent scout, demonstrating thoughtful good judgement of both character and qualification, an important asset in team-building for large projects.

The following statement, published in an article on the firm's work, is important, as it explains the firm's approach to organizational structure (or lack of it) in the design area, the role of the mentor and the degree of freedom employees were allowed to pursue different ideas and attitudes. While it was written by Pratt in 1961, it was approved by the partners, and represents clearly the situation as it was evolving, which set 'the' example for Ron Thom and the others on how a practice should operate. It was the only model they knew.

Thompson, Berwick, Pratt [is the current version of the firm that] was established in 1908 and is thus one of the oldest firms in Vancouver. The present firm bears only a slight resemblance to itself in the original state except in one important attitude: the acceptance of the principle of change. Great freedom exists within the firm for both staff and partners. It is difficult to find a reigning attitude either on architecture specifically, or on its practice. This does not mean that strong attitudes do not exist, or that at various times certain attitudes do not emerge more strongly than others. But it does mean a general suspicion of dogma to which all buildings and people creating buildings must conform. Over the years, various systems to even out architectural design have been tried, usually with short-lived success. Without exception these have been abandoned or greatly modified to accommodate individuals and situations. While this belief in the individual has at times caused dark spots in performance as well as bright ones, it allows for another kind of order to exist. This is the gradual change and progression that comes about through the influence of one person on others, rather than the control of one person over others. This is perhaps a slower means of arriving at real architectural excellence but, for ourselves, we know of no other way towards a healthy architecture.[4]

This policy and the volume of work acted as a magnet to draw the best talent from across the city and from farther afield. With the mix of talent and experience thus available to them the partners found it easy to assign the most promising individuals to head up small staff teams on a temporary basis to take on different building types. There were groups doing schools and groups for health care facilities, university building (the firm had the exclusive contract for the whole UBC campus expansion until 1957), banks and commercial buildings, and still others for functional activities such as specifications and field supervision. These in turn were clustered under the general supervision of the partners, and new partners were promoted from within the firm as the volume of work increased. There was a tendency to separate the "bread and butter" projects which were mostly repetitive (such as schools), from the more prestigious, exotic or otherwise highly visible projects. These latter ones usually became Pratt's responsibility. Houses were treated differently— when they stemmed from clients of one of the partners, that person picked whomever he wanted to work on it, and it was done (somewhat reluctantly as they were never profitable) as an office project in regular time, or alternatively and more usually as overtime commitments by interested staff.

Within this flexible framework, there was every opportunity for the energetic and capable to move around from group to group to get extra and more varied experience, working in the field on a little or a large project to get experience in contract supervision and to develop close relations with clients—a formula for takeoff into a separate practice. Although the atmosphere was highly competitive, the senior partners relied on and favoured the self-starters who understood the implicit message coded in the firm's policy. These individuals had no doubt that this firm was winning the most interesting commissions in the city and was open to experimentation with the modernist ideas of the day. During the 1950s, for up-and-coming young architects in Vancouver, it was indeed the preferred office, and a truly happy place to work. Ron Thom thrived in this situation. He could see interesting opportunities and avenues open to him to develop his knowledge of architecture and practise, and he could see that his goal, to become an architect, was within the realm of possibility. All he had to do was work at it.

5 Apprenticeship

WHILE THOM WAS ASSIGNED the office-boy's job on his first day as an apprentice, when it was discovered that he could produce perspective drawings and render them in watercolour at great speed (he had been practising for the year since that ill-fated watercolour rendering for Ned Pratt), he was immediately in demand to illustrate the work coming off the job-captains' boards. However, he did this with some frustration, as he had no intention of spending his time as a delineator of somebody else's designs. He saw quickly that he would have to get as much experience as possible in design if he was to develop significantly.

For the first few years, the outlet for Thom was to design houses on his own time. He had just completed his own house, and it, along with the Bobaks' house next door, had attracted a lot of attention because of a series of highly entertaining radio interviews that Molly Bobak had done on the CBC in 1950, describing both families' trials and tribulations with unfinished houses and new babies. During the construction of these houses, Ron had also designed two other houses, one for his brother-in-law, and another for Peter Aspell, a painter friend from art school. All of these houses were on the same street in North Vancouver. (Unfortunately all except the the Aspell house have been demolished.) They were experiments with post-and-beam construction with tongued-and-grooved cedar plank roof decks, standard 2 x 4 stud walls with cedar siding and glass. These houses were small—under 1000 square feet—and very inexpensive, with complete material and equipment costs in the $5000-6000 range. Most of them were at least partially built by their owners and friends.

Molly Bobak tells the story that, "on Peters Road [where they were building] if anybody bought a lot on the street within view of their two houses, Ron would be over there trying to persuade them to let him design their house so it would help unify the street. 'I'll do it free, just so long as you build it the way I tell you to.' He built four houses this way!!"[1]

Berwick and Pratt liked these early houses and liked the enterprise Thom showed in their production. To foster his further development they started to assign to him some larger houses to him for their own clients, backing him up with experienced technical and production staff.

Bob Berwick had developed a large clientele for suburban houses and prided himself that he could design the plan and elevations, draw a perspective and a few details and fit them all on not more than two sheets of 11"x 17" tracing paper. He lectured the staff constantly that that was all that was needed to get it built. He had several houses going at once for many years, and he used to supervise their construction on his way to work in the morning, no doubt drawing the missing details on the back of an envelope.

In contrast, Pratt's work was more tectonic. He was fascinated by the construction process, and he sought ways and means to simplify on-site work by the pre-cutting of structural materials and the pre-assembly of panelized components and window frames, thereby reducing end costs. His plans were all developed on a structural module—a dimensional grid. His earlier work was based on post-and-beam construction, usually showing the posts in the exterior wall and exploiting the opportunity to use large glass areas to fill the whole space between the posts in certain rooms.

Thom became interested in Pratt's work, because he had experimented with post-and-beam construction in his own house. Pratt assigned him to design and supervise the multi-level Copp house in Vancouver (completed in 1951), and the Mayhew house in Victoria (completed in 1957), both of which were early examples of the flat-roofed post-and-beam houses that at the time were considered "radical" or "leading edge" by the press, and very disturbing to their clients' conservative neighbours in their make-believe "Tudor" manors.

Part of Thom's early success with clients came from the fact that he was a very good listener. At a lecture in Vancouver in 1949, Neutra had described in detail his interviewing technique for house clients, and it had made a strong impression on Thom. At that time Neutra was researching his book *Survival Through Design* [2] and was in contact with a number of scientists from several fields. From information he had acquired, he was experimenting with a technique which involved getting his clients' reaction to a carefully developed set of questions regarding their requirements as users of the home-to-be.

Arthur Drexler, in a book on Neutra's work, makes some perceptive comments on another facet of this technique, hinting at the manipulative nature of it: *Neutra's planning is remarkable for its undogmatic, perfectly straightforward dealing with his clients' preferences. Neutra made much of getting to know his clients, subjecting them to long interviews and detailed questionnaires. The latter must often have kept them busy for the few days he needed to design a house. In any case, there is no reason to doubt his sympathetic curiosity about the clients' lives. What is striking, however, is the similarity of the solutions to what each of them may have believed were uniquely personal requirements.* [3]

While Thom never used this elaborate technique, the importance of the interview and listening with eyes wide open was indelibly imprinted on him. He would spend long hours discussing requirements with his clients, but designing and drawing plans, sections and perspectives on the spot, with frequent reference to slides or magazines illustrating forms, materials, colours, decoration and other elements of

houses and sites to get his ideas across. These discussions, by their very intensity as a learning experience, were also engaging and irresistible to the clients as their very own house became visible. Broadcaster Barbara Frum, a long-time client of Thom's, described this experience: *As he told us at that first meeting, he loved doing houses, enjoyed working closely with clients on the intimate sum of personal details that a house is . . . Ron was an artist who made a refined aesthetic out of unrefinement, a master of the difference between complexity and fussiness. He taught us to love raw surfaces and the natural, to recognize harmonious proportions, how good it is to sleep and eat close to the floor, to be wrapped in a cocoon of a dark room, punctuated by the sparkle of tiny beams of light, how everything went together if you knew what you were doing—how many steps made a walk inviting, how many made a destination too far, and how broad and deep these treads must be—which he'd dance out for us to teach the difference, striding up and down across the floor.* [4]

Thom's professional relationship with Barbara Frum and her husband, Murray, did not commence until the mid-1970s, but it lasted for fifteen years—a rare example of the architect finding the perfect client who is willing to submit to and encourage the near-tyranny of his intrusion into their privacy and life style. Even at the early stage of his career, Thom had acquired a reputation for his sensitivity to clients' requirements as well as his design talent, and he made among his clients long-term friends and advocates who sent him still more house clients.

Initially, Thom attempted to follow through with the necessary production drawings for these projects by himself, but he soon discovered that there were not enough hours in the day, on top of all his other obligations and responsibilities. As well, he frequently found himself beyond his depth regarding the technical resolution of his designs. He turned to his friends on staff, and several of them were interested enough in his ideas to be willing to 'moonlight,' to do the drawings on their own time at night in order to see these projects built and learn in the process. As one of them says: "there was no overtime pay . . . the reward was pride, or occasionally, Ned [Pratt] might arrive at two in the morning with a can of beer and give you a pat on the back."[5] Thom soon had a following of supporters in the office who wanted to see him flourish and develop, and who helped him with his studies and provided all kinds of advice to keep him out of trouble at this early stage of his career. When he started the second four-year term of his indenture, he began to study seriously for the registration examinations, joining with others to hire technical consultants to teach them the more elusive subjects.

THOM'S EARLY HOUSES illustrate how quickly his many talents had started to come together, and they reveal something of his thinking process. The Copp house and the later Mayhew house are both larger and more refined versions of the post-and-beam house, similar to the one he built for himself in 1949. The Mayhew house, which he did working closely with Pratt, reflects the indoor-outdoor California lifestyle as represented by the plan of the Kaufman house of Richard Neutra in its separate wings for particular clusters of family activities. The Woodward house was one of the first clearly derivative projects originating from the "Usonian" series of houses completed by Frank Lloyd Wright[6] about the same time and based on a similar modular grid, which can be seen in the structure and the window walls. The Bennett house, built around a courtyard, was the earliest large and relatively expensive house that Thom worked on, exploring the full formal possibilities of the big, sheltering, wide-eaved hipped roof.

8

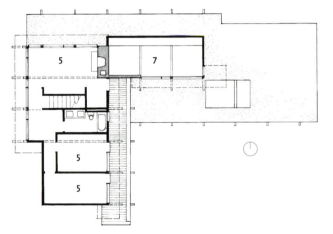

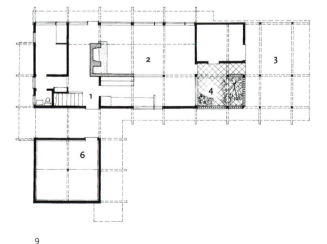

9

Copp house

Figure 8
The north all-glass wall of the living room, as seen from the slope below, faces Burrard Inlet and the mountains of North and West Vancouver.

Figure 9
Plans: upper level (top) and ground level (bottom).
1 entry
2 living/dining room
3 carport
4 patio
5 bedrooms
6 workshop/storage
7 space over living room

Figure 10
The entrance from the driveway.

10

These houses all reflect the profound influence of the California work of Frank Lloyd Wright, Harwell Hamilton Harris, Richard Neutra and Rudolph Schindler on Thom as he experimented with principles and features of "modern" architecture as illustrated in their work. They also demonstrate how facile Thom had become in adapting them to quite different client programs and siting opportunities in Vancouver with its very different climate.

These features included the following:

- the open plan, where many of the expected partitions between rooms are left out, allowing the space to flow from one area to the other, and to the outside, but particularly between the exterior and interior living and dining areas, the kitchen and circulation areas. A massive fireplace, visible from all parts of the open area, provided the symbolic "heart" of the house—in the British Columbia climate a welcome extra source of heat during the damp, dark parts of the year.
- the use of a continuous horizontal line or band at door height which locates the head of most of the windows and doors (approximately seven feet above the floor), and provides a launching point for higher spaces shaped by the underside of the roof, whether it is flat or sloped.
- the strip window—a continuous horizontal band of windows, usually set under or over the horizontal band at the door height. The sill is not necessarily continuous at one level, and may rise or drop to accommodate the placement of cabinetry or furniture on the inside, or site variations on the outside. The sill could also be sloped to follow the profile of an abutting roof or to capture a view. The strip integrated sheets of glass, casement windows and structural support for the roof. By careful arrangement of the structure, keeping it away from the corner, the strip window could turn the corner, and the two adjacent panes of glass could be glued together to form the corner.
- the use of large sheets of glass as exterior walls, and other applications of floor-to-ceiling glass windows and corners to give continuity between inside and outside, and to open up views of sweeping landscapes or up-close views of trees or other landscape features. In the 1950s, before the development of double-glazed windows this was very daring!
- the wide overhang of the roof, which provides sun-shading and weather protection to the wall below, and allows casement windows or sliding doors to be open for ventilation even in rainy weather. Wright and Harris favoured the hip roof, with the underside of the overhang, the soffit, constructed as a flat surface set at the level of the horizontal band and the head of the strip window. Neutra and Schindler more often used the flat roof. All of them varied the width of the overhang according to the height of the window below as required for precise shading during the hottest days of the year, pushing the overhang to the limits of cantilever construction to shade full-height glass walls and doors onto patios.

Copp house

Figure 11
The living room. The square table and large chairs are prototypes for furniture Thom designed for Massey College in 1962.

12

13

Mayhew house

Figure 12
The water side which overlooks the yacht basin and the Olympic mountains in the Strait of Juan de Fuca.

Figure 13
The fenced garden side as seen from the upper level.

Figure 14
The living room.

Figure 15
Plan, 1957. This early zoned plan for a large one-storey family house is influenced by the pinwheel planning of a large house built by Richard Neutra in 1947, the Kaufman house.

Figure 16
A diagrammatic plan of Richard Neutra's Kaufman house, Palm Springs, 1947. It shows the separated functional units located and oriented to provide privacy and freedom of access.

1 *social area*
2 *owners' suite*
2a *parents' suite*
3 *guest suite*
3a *children's suite*
3b *family room*
4 *kitchen/services*
5 *garage*
6 *pool/recreation*

14

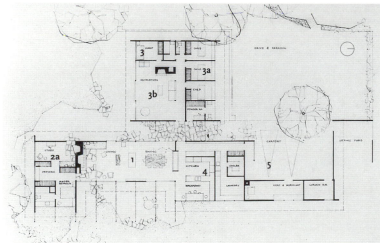

15

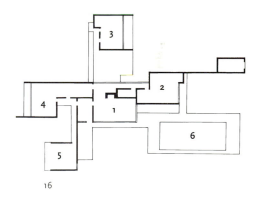

16

Woodward/Trier-Pevecz house

Figure 17
The west wall. The modular construction and the floor to ceiling glass are reminiscent of the Usonian houses of Frank Lloyd Wright.

Figure 18
The southwest corner of the living room. The vertical window frame, each complete with its own venetian blind on the inside, is set directly in the notched columns and headers on a 32 inch module to line up with the 16 inch spacing of the roof joists. The horizontal line that separates the clerestory windows from the long vertical windows below is the edge of a light-shelf which extends into the big room to illuminate the higher ceiling. The corner window is glass, butt-jointed and glued.

18

THE ISSUE OF SITING was a subject of continuing discussion. Neutra had produced a little book, *The Mystery and Reality of the Site*,[7] that struck a chord with Thom, as did the work of John Yeon of Portland, Oregon—a location with a similar climate and landscape features to Vancouver. The siting issue is also related to the quality of natural light, which is affected by the hours of sunshine available at a particular latitude, and the position of elements in the landscape itself, particularly trees.

Sometime in the mid-1950s I once asked both Arthur Erickson and Ron Thom separately where they would place a house on the same site in West Vancouver. The lot lay on a slope facing southwest that was completely forested and therefore private, and which had a major granite outcrop that provided a natural ledge or platform and a magnificent view overlooking the entrance to Howe Sound and Georgia Strait. Neither of them would touch the rock. Erickson said he would create a clearing for the house on the forest side of the outcrop to make it possible to open the house to the sun and the sky. The main floor level would be set slightly lower than the rock platform in order to provide a foregound for the view. He would then build the house with large glass areas, and paint the interiors white so as to distribute the light through the whole interior. Thom said he would build the house in the trees near the rock with the least possible disturbance to the site, and approach it from a level above or below in such a way as to come across it in the trees but not be able to see all of it. You would experience the site as a sequence of close up and longer views as you moved through the interior of the house that revealed the features of the forest and terminated at the rock ledge with the full sweep of the view of the water. He suggested he would resort to clerestory windows to get filtered sky light and views up into the trees, and windows of varying size to provide 'framed pictures' of the forest, including glimpses of the water through the trees. Many of Thom's built houses are arranged in this way, and they are sometimes dark and moody on an overcast or rainy day, but they provide an intimate relationship to the site in all its seasonal variations.

The more than forty houses that Thom had produced in Vancouver by the late 1950s were radically different to the ranch-style bungalows provided to the market by builders of the day, and they quickly attracted attention, leading to further commissions and awards. He continued his experimentation, gradually developing a distinctive formal vocabulary suitable to the wide variety of siting conditions and climates of the Vancouver area.

THOM HAD STUDIED the work of the California architects in the available books and magazines, but he had also seen that work at first hand on a field-trip in 1952. It is always an educational experience to view a building seen before only in photographs and plans, as the reality is never the same as the expectation. It is either bigger, or smaller, or the photos have screened out some undesirable feature of the site or context that intrudes on its 'presence', which to have acknowledged it would have exposed a flaw in the architect's decisions. The experience confirms that architects are human, too. More importantly, it forces the questions, "why did he do that?" and "how did he do that?" and "why is this so wonderful/awful?"—the fundamental questions that lead to a critical judgement that changes one's view of that architect or of the building. It also generates a sense of how difficult it is to make a building, and provides a measure for your own work, development and self-confidence.

Bennett/Hawes house

Figure 19
The north side facing Burrard inlet and the mountain view.

This big house has been completely reconstructed as required to bring it up to 1990 codes and market standards for equipment, safety and convenience, while, at the same time, exercising great care to follow the intent of the original working drawings. This has been done with superb detailing and craftsmanship.

21

Bennett/Hawes house

Figure 20
The entry hall, and the walk
past the courtyard to the
carport. The door decorations
are new work.

Figure 21
The all-glass corner window
and the soaring hip-roof
overhang, a flat cedar soffit.

Ron Thom made several field trips with Fred Hollingsworth, another disciple of the same architects, to see particular buildings. Hollingsworth was an old friend of Thom from high school days, and he was also an apprentice in the TBP office. They were both self taught, so these trips provided the verification of the actual quality of the work they had only seen in photographs until then. Therefore their discussions had a synergistic effect on their ideas about architecture, resulting in a great deal of experimentation with their earlier, low-cost, smaller houses in their 'moonlighting' days.

By the mid-1950s, Thom's growing self-confidence and convictions were much in evidence in the office, as he became more critical and outspoken about the work going on around him. While serious and well-intentioned, he was not known for tact, and he did not suffer fools, or those he considered fools, lightly. There were many well-educated and capable architects on the staff as well as very experienced and knowledgeable draftsmen, and in a serious discussion about architectural ideas or technical matters with these people whom he respected Thom listened carefully, keeping the subject open and alive, learning from them. Ned Pratt recalls that "he was very quick to pick up a book reference and to follow it up and re-open the discussion when he had digested it, whether it was a visual or textual reference."[8]

Another observer, John Wallace, notes: *when Ron held forth, he was forceful and articulate as long as a topic interested him. He was a lightning rod, . . . he attracted people and kept them there . . . he was not at all one-sided, he had the capability to listen and step in . . . creating a platform for people to talk to. However, he could get testy if it got beyond his ability to deal with it.*[9]

As the postwar generation of architects in the office matured, it was inevitable that Thom would find his confidence in his convictions challenged and occasionally shaken up by the arguments offered in these discussions, and at some point he began to realize that he may have missed something important by lacking formal education in architecture. Self-taught knowledge is usually unstructured and is not systematic, but it has the benefit of immediate relevance, and hence has a powerful and frequently indelible impact. Nevertheless, Thom became self-conscious and self-deprecating about his 'lack of education.' He had learned to joke about it, putting on a cynical front, but it gnawed at him throughout his career. In later years he put another slant on it, confiding to a friend that he felt he "was penalized for not coming through university."[10]

Friday afternoon was set aside at the office as a vehicle for informal contact and exchange between staff and the partners, consultants, visitors and sometimes clients who happened to be there at the time. Ron Thom seldom missed these occasions. It was an unpredictable and potentially volatile mix of people and drink that could stir up serious discussion, strong feelings, arguments, serious poker games, music, ongoing party-fever or a mix of any or all of them at once. After the first hour, the group would boil down to those who wanted to keep it going, mostly those who enjoyed drinking and the challenge of either discussion or cards. It was on these extended occasions that it became clear to his friends that Ron Thom had the beginnings of a serious drinking problem.

6 Becoming an Architect

THE PARTNERS RECOGNIZED they had a valuable asset in Thom and started to assign him to larger projects which would stretch his design and planning skills, and to provide him with the staff backup for technical support. Increasingly, in the work he was doing other than housing, one can see evidence of a search for different forms, a wider palette of materials as he got involved with larger buildings and more permanent construction, while developing an overall fluency of composition and expression. He was also getting experience working in several multi-disciplinary teams, without which it is impossible to build complex buildings. The more interesting examples from this period include the Automobile Sales Showroom for Clarke Simpkins, the Plywood Research Laboratory in North Vancouver, and the Delport Inn in Richmond.

In the mid-1950s, he was assigned to work on two important projects which, as they materialized, became a kind of two-year preliminary examination of his ability to integrate design throughout a large complex project, set for him and two or three others as they were completing their apprenticeship term and preparing to sit for their registration exams.

THE BC ELECTRIC COMPANY, the province's dominant private-sector utility company, was, in 1952, in the process of major expansion of its hydro-electric power generation development and distribution system to meet the anticipated rapidly growing demands of the Province of British Columbia. In need of office space, the company (re-named BC Hydro in 1962) made the decision to build two highly visible general-purpose office buildings, one each in prominent locations in Vancouver and Victoria, to house its principal management operations.

In Vancouver, the company had purchased a city block on the edge of downtown as the location for its new office building, a substation and works division, anticipating the development of the central core of the city. The substation had been designed by its engineering staff, and building was about to start when the president, Dal Grauer, concerned about the image of the corporation, had second thoughts. He consulted Ned Pratt, a close friend, to advise him on the building's design. Pratt pointed out that *the proposed design for the new substation was identical to that they had built on Main Street, and that the corporation was about to hide some very interesting looking and expensive equipment in a neo-Classical building that might be construed by the public and the adjacent churches as a mausoleum, and that would probably not project the image the president had in mind.*[1]

Grauer told Pratt to fix it up.

Inspired by thoughts of a Mondrian painting, Pratt decided that the front wall facing Burrard Street (a main traffic artery) should be made of large sheets of glass in a minimal steel grid to show off the "guts" of the building, and that the equipment so exposed should be painted in strong colours. His recommendation was approved and the building was modified accordingly. Pratt consulted with Bert Binning on the colours, and the resulting product, while owing little to Mondrian, was an immediate popular success.

Pratt was also asked to advise on the siting of the new head-office building, which was to be a twenty-five storey tower, the first of that height in Vancouver. He recommended that the site next to the substation, the highest land on the downtown peninsula, was also the best of three available sites under consideration. This was agreed, but when Grauer then proposed to his Board that Pratt should be awarded the contract for the tower to start right away, they expressed concerns that the TBP firm did not have the expertise to do it. Pratt was given time

34

22

Clarke Simpkins

Figure 22
An auto dealer's showroom.

23

Plywood Research Laboratory

Figure 23
The roof is constructed of stressed skin plywood polyhedrons, weatherproofed with a fiberglass skin.

Figure 24
The interior workspace

24

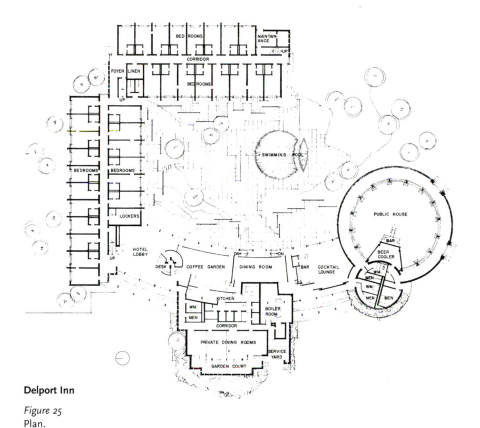

Delport Inn

Figure 25
Plan.

to assemble a team and make a detailed proposal. He travelled to San Francisco and New York before he settled on Fred Severud, an internationally respected structural engineer, who agreed to come from New York with two other consultants with state-of-the-art expertise in mechanical and electrical systems for high-rise buildings. With this assurance, the Board approved the appointment of TBP with Pratt as "partner-in-charge" directly responsible to the president for the design and implementation of the Vancouver tower and the Victoria office building. They also agreed that the Victoria building should proceed first and be used as a 'test bed' for innovative ideas for the head office building.

Working closely with Pratt, Ron Thom and Bob Gibson, another apprentice, along with Otto Safir (the Vancouver structural engineer who would do all the detailed development of the building structures), developed the preliminary programmatic analysis and siting studies for the Victoria building. These indicated that it should be a six-to-eight storey, narrow, linear building located on the long north side of the corner site provided, with the offices facing south, and a continuous corridor on the north side. This decision saved huge mature trees on the south side of the property, which provided some sun screening. But more importantly, it created a park-like setting at the intersection of the two major streets, Pandora and Blanshard on the south and west sides of the site respectively. Design proceeded on a simple reinforced concrete frame with full bay-width strip windows for each floor between the columns. The innovation suggested by the structural consultant, Fred Severud, was to introduce a fifty-foot, column-free span for the floor slabs, allowing maximum planning flexibility for each floor. The distinguishing feature of the building is the sun-control device on the windows on the south and

26

27

BC Electric, Victoria

Figure 26
The south face of the office building showing the aluminum sunshades, unfortunately painted black. This was later corrected, but they were repainted white, rather than reverting to the natural finish of the aluminum. The cast-in-place frieze at the roof line illustrates Thom's interest in decoration, which appears often in his work.

BC Electric tower, Vancouver

Figure 27
A Ron Thom drawing of the south face of the 22-storey office building for BC Electric, Vancouver. This was one of the first studies of the final form of the tower and the lower floor components.

west elevations. It consists of three horizontal aluminum louvres, curved in cross-section, and supported on brackets across the top half of the strip windows of each floor. A few decorative gestures were added, including the use of recessed cross-forms like rosettes cast into the concrete, and the use of 1"x 1" reveals to articulate the outside corners of the structural frame. Pratt again brought in Binning to advise on colour and interior finish materials. The modest scale and elegant proportions of the building—a simple box—together with the directness, simplicity and functional good sense of the overall project, make it an excellent building which has never received the attention it deserved. (Several years ago it was sold to the provincial government and integrated into a larger building complex, and since has suffered from changes in use and insensitive colour schemes.)

The larger Vancouver project was much more complex. The site rises to the southwest corner, giving it prominence and a spectacular view over the harbour and mountains. This high side of the site was designated for the office tower. On the ground floor it would connect downhill to the substation. The lower level area of the remaining site was reserved for future development, to be used initially for parking, workshops and maintenance equipment. Dal Grauer, who was out to build a "flagship" building, had agreed with Pratt's selection of the site because of its dominant position in the downtown area and its future potential. He told Pratt to "build it to prevent expropriation. Make it as expensive [to do] as possible!"[2]

The architects and consultants decided to fast-track the whole development, starting with the remaining engineering projects for the site, a decision which allowed the architectural team to start the design of the tower in 1955 as the Victoria pro-

ject was nearing completion. Because the fast-track technique was new to TBP, Pratt expanded and reorganized his team in Vancouver, which then included Thom and three others, bringing in Dave Hickman, by then a new junior partner, to negotiate the schedules and coordinate them with the contractual aspects of the project, pacing the architectural work accordingly.

The preliminary design that evolved was for a rectangular tower of twenty stories above the main floor concourse. The latter spread out to connect to other buildings on the site, and to house a cafeteria and other amenities. The elevators were in the centre of the tower building, which, together with the other service rooms required, formed a central core for the full height of the building and projected through the roof to form a high penthouse to house the machinery for the elevators and other mechanical equipment. Safir proposed to build the core of reinforced concrete. This core would thus provide both seismic and windbracing stability, and leave the outer small columns to support only the remaining twenty-seven-foot outer band of the office floors. The space between these small columns could then be enclosed by a lightweight aluminum-and-glass curtain wall.

Pratt and his design team, however, were not enamoured of the "cereal box" form of the tower, and they were concerned to give the project a unique and memorable image. Keeping within the functional constraints of the preliminary design, they started to explore ways and means to model the form. By careful planning they were able to reduce the area of the core of the building, ending up with a tapered space wide at the central elevator core, and narrow at the two ends. The corridor which surrounds this core was reduced in length as a result, improving the floor area efficiency—that is the ratio of useable (potentially rentable) office space to that required for access and services. This pulled in the office space at the ends, and the result is the 'lozenge' shape of the final tower plan. Thom's first sketches of this building show its handsome profile and overall form, and also illustrate the first exploration of the form of the base floor. This was larger than the tower floors, and hence extended out from under the tower to connect with the substation in one corner, and to the surrounding streets.

The solution was a logical statement arising directly from functional necessitites, subtley modelled to improve the street-level spaces around the building and the pedestrian's relationship to the building and the street. When discussing the BCE tower other architects frequently suggest that the form is derived from another lozenge-shaped tower, the Pirelli Building in Milan, which actually did not appear in the architectural press until after the BCE building was completed. That building is ten stories higher, with almost exactly the same tower floor area, but its bearing-wall structure, of necessity, is radically different. It was this feature, designed by the great Italian engineer, Pier Luigi Nervi with the architect, Gio Ponti, that attracted wide publicity at the time. While the BCE building did not attract the same publicity, it preceded that building, and is an original solution.

Once the bulk form of the building was settled, the team moved on to resolve the detailed design and development of all aspects of the building. There were many innovative technical features, including using off-peak generation of electrical energy to heat hot water stored for use the following day to heat the tower. The long search for an acceptable material to cover the large concrete surfaces of the service core, areas of the external and internal concrete walls of lobbies and the foundation and planting areas was resolved by a suggestion from a visiting architect that "mosaic tile is what you need—go to Italy and have them make it to your specs, build in the designs you want."[3] The team agreed, and Bert Binning was brought in again to work with Thom to develop proposals for the colour and patterning of this material, and for the final design of the areas around the building. With Pratt, they settled on a repetitive design motif based on the lozenge-shaped plan of the building which was used at different scales in specific areas as features. Layout drawings for these areas were all worked out in Vancouver, and Binning went to Italy to settle the final colours and any outstanding details.

Florence Knoll, probably the leading interior designer of the day, was flown in from New York to "do up" the Executive floor, which, according to Dave Hickman, *led to a showdown between her and Binning about her proposed colour scheme: she wanted white walls and feature panels in primary colours [red, yellow and blue]; he wanted "west coast" colours [blue, green, and grey]. She ended up doing the walls of the executive floor in natural wood, and was then awarded the contract for the furnishing of the rest of the building.*[4]

The lozenge motif was cast in place in the huge, cantilevered reinforced concrete canopies over the entrance doors, and it was used as a shape to define the outline of large elongated holes to lighten the weight of a cantilevered concrete cornice flying over the edge of the building above the twentieth floor. As a final feature, twenty-storey vertical V-shape lanterns were built onto the centre of both ends of the building, reputedly so that "Tom Ingeldow, the vice-president, could see it at night from his cabin-cruiser lying off Point Grey!"[5]

By a later decision, all the lights in the building were left on through the night, so that the whole

BC Electric tower

Figure 28
This 1993 photo shows the BC Electric tower as built (the name was changed later to the "BC Hydro" building). The building was sold the next year for conversion to condominium housing.

building became a beacon seen from many areas of Vancouver. While this seemed contrary to the effort put into the cost-saving energy-conservation features of the building, the public relations pundits had prevailed over these practical considerations, basing their argument on a more simplistic 'efficiency' rationale-of-the-day, namely, that 'it is cheaper to leave a flourescent light on continuously than to keep switching it on and off'. The client was, after all, selling electricity.

By 1958 the high quality of the finished building, and its high visibility, established Thompson, Berwick, Pratt and Ned Pratt as the leading firm and architect in Vancouver. "He was seen in the city as the anchor in the firm and taken very seriously in his own client world."[6] The national awareness of the firm's increasing design prominence as a result of this building and the number of Massey Medals the firm had won led to Pratt's appointment to the international jury for the Toronto City Hall Competition in 1958, and to the prestigious task force set up by Central Mortgage and Housing Corporation which, after touring Canada in 1960, was to advise the federal government on housing policy.

The BC Electric tower was ahead of its time in Vancouver in that the economic boom had by 1958 produced urban sprawl, not concentration, and the buildup of a high density urban core did not really get underway in that city until the 1980s. The firm never did another project like it. Nevertheless, this building was the first of the new generation of office buildings built in Vancouver in the postwar period, and it set the pace for elegance and quality in subsequent development. It may be that its greatest contribution to the urban environment is the precedent it set for the way a high building meets the ground, and the thoughtful use of planting and paving to create places for people to sit and enjoy the sunshine and the passing scene, features which have made parts of downtown Vancouver very pleasant for pedestrians.

FOR RON THOM it was obviously an important learning experience. He had worked hard and made a major contribution to the BC Electric projects and was beginning to get anxious about his own future in the firm. The senior partners had taken on four new junior partners in 1955 to assist with the administration of this rapidly growing firm (Roy Jessiman, John Dayton, Fred Brodie and Dave Hickman). All of them were near the same age as Thom, and his self-esteem had reached the stage where he was wondering whose contribution was more important to the future of the firm. He was also beginning to see himself challenging Pratt's leadership role in design.

In 1957, he had written and passed his final examinations for registration, and he became a registered architect. The following year, another building he had worked on, the CKWX Radio Station, was awarded a Massey Medal (silver) in the 1958 Massey Awards Competition, the only one the firm won in that round. This was the sixth medal for a building for which Thom had been the lead designer, of the eight medals the firm had won to that date. The medals had started to carry considerable weight with the public because they were well publicized nationally. At this point the firm finally offered him a partnership, which he accepted with alacrity, undoubtedly wondering why it had taken so long.

Over the next five years, as a new partner, Thom continued to work at the same intensity, becoming more outspoken and critical—Pratt says "he was becoming cheeky"[7]—and also temperamental, a sure formula for conflict. It did not take long to surface.

The distinctive nature of Thom's work, particularly

his houses, stood out, but his other work was already attracting both local and national attention. Inevitably, the members of the public and the media wanted to know who had "designed" which particular project. To paraphrase their attitude: 'We want to know who is the true genius, the artist whose imagination and skill permeates every aspect and detail of that building'. Having become a partner, Thom was finally in a position to respond directly to that attention, as he could now take full credit for the design of the projects on which he worked. He saw himself precisely in the role as paraphrased above, and any person who has been a client for a house he designed would confirm to this day that this paraphrased comment described exactly what he was, and what he demonstrated from first contact through construction. To take this position now that he was working on large and more prestigious projects, however, put him in direct conflict with Pratt and his partners. For them loyalty to the firm was everything. To paraphrase their position: 'We all contribute in our own way to every project, and each of us works for the greater glory of the whole'. Unfortunately, while Thom was clear about his loyalty to the firm, the media frequently saw it differently in their quest to publicize the 'designer' as a celebrity. This became a source of great annoyance, particularly to Pratt.

Arguments over attribution of credit are endemic in architectural practice. Many firms have written rules and procedures to handle these situations. Thompson, Berwick, Pratt had only the statement of principle about 'loyalty.' While the principals of many firms will tolerate attribution of credit when the project has truly been the work of one person with minor assistance, they will get very upset if it is applied to a major building which has been the result of a complicated team effort.

BC Electric tower

Figure 29
The entrance to the tower, and the seating area between the building and the street sidewalk, on the sunny side of the building. The mosaic tile patterns are based on the lozenge shape of the tower floor plan, and the same pattern is used to position the beams in the concrete canopy structure, but at a larger scale.

In recent years the tendency is to acknowledge the whole project team, listing in order, the partner-in-charge, the managing architect (if different), the lead-designer (a registered architect), and the various team members in order of seniority—some of the last of these not yet registered architects. This list is followed by another of the various consultants. The positive effect on morale in the offices that adhere to this practice is very noticeable.

If that approach had been taken on the BC Electric tower project, Ron Thom would, at the least, have been eligible to be credited with the lead design-architect role, as he had become a registered architect in 1957, a year before completion of the project, and it was the perception in the office that he was indeed filling that role. Not being so acknowledged was a source of continuing bitterness on Thom's part toward Pratt. Probably the most publicized building the firm ever produced, the BC Electric tower can be seen in many articles and books presenting the most notable and best Canadian architecture. Ironically, it is almost always credited to Ron Thom, with or without reference to the Vancouver firm.

SINCE THOM HAD BECOME A PARTNER, the time he had previously devoted to study for the examinations he directed into design, pushing for more and more responsibility. He was driven by his idealism and the need to prove to himself that he was the best. Work was where he could excel, and there was a continuous supply of it to feed his addiction. At home, after the birth of a second child, he had found himself unprepared for the additional complications of two more children in the next few years. As these complications arose, he became more impatient and frustrated in his role as a parent. He would frequently boil over in a burst of temper that invited responsive retaliation and strained his relationship with Chris and the children still further.

While Chris carried the main burden of raising the family, she had done so to this point at the sacrifice of her own development as an artist, grounds for considerable resentment. By 1960, she had had enough and moved out, taking the children to Victoria. Ron and Chris were divorced in 1961.

7 Houses West

In Vancouver, in the period 1957-63, Thom had more than thirty houses in overlapping stages of design and construction over and above the other work he was doing for Thompson, Berwick, Pratt. These include his most mature work among the many houses he built in the West. To produce them a very efficient small team coalesced around him, headed by Dick Mann and Bob Burniston. At different times it included several architects in the firm, all good designers themselves, who admired Ron and wanted to work with him on houses for a while. Among them were Barry Downs, Fred Hollingsworth, Dick Archambault and Bob Boal. As some of these houses were very large and carried generous budgets (by comparison with earlier houses) the opportunity was opened to push structural and constructional conventions, to build complex hip roofs with soaring cantilever corners, to explore and refine ideas about siting, form, space, the use of materials, detailing, cabinetry, day and night lighting, and to explore different formal vocabularies. In an article in *Canadian Architect* Thom wrote: *What suggests the form of a particular house? . . We all begin via the process of eclecticism . . . this is a natural and proper phase in the learning process. Every child learns by imitation. It is only in the mature creative person that this process is replaced by his own observation and synthesis.*

Every architect has thought his way of arranging things was particularly simple. Simplicity is one's own sense of unity, where pattern is revealed out of apparent disorder. The creative mind looks for unexpected likenesses.

Each house is developed on its own geometrical figure. This is as elementary in architecture as it is in music, and it serves to keep the grammar clear. But this does not explain why the form of each is as it is.

Form can only result from one's own idea of the relationship between everything involved. An architect, no less than an artist, should be willing to fly in the face of what is established, and to create not what is acceptable but what will become accepted. Phases of work tend to run in long cycles rather than jumping from pillar to post. This latter pattern implies continued eclecticism and art for art's sake where style feeds off itself. This can only produce buildings that are meaningless for all concerned and leave nothing of substance behind. Architecture is always capable of cannibalizing itself.

The pressure to change one's own work builds up gradually as one kind of form is pushed to the point where it is no longer adequate to answer the needs of expanding awareness. Hence, looked at this way, form is nothing more than a vehicle of expression.

New forms give the impression sometimes that they arrive suddenly. This is a false impression. Their arrival may be sudden enough, but the pressure that makes form is incessant. Ideas do not come out of thin air. If an architect does not alter form quickly or easily, his form is probably more related to vogue than intent.[1]

Thom met with the clients and worked up the preliminary design, usually late at night, turning it over to Dick Mann or one of the others for further development over which he kept a sharp eye. Bob Burniston supervised the production of the contract documents and the construction. Because many of the houses were similar, the team evolved a series of standard plans and details for bathroom and kitchen components, and other storage cabinets and fittings. Inevitably, as in the case of Neutra and Wright, several prototypical plans emerged for family houses in similar siting conditions (for example, large corner lots in the city), which were then refined by their adaptation to the character of the site and to specific family needs. With the volume of work they were handling and Thom's other responsibilities, in an emergency Mann and Burniston could and did turn out a few "Thom" houses that are almost impossible

to separate from those Thom stood over personally, which is perhaps an ironic demonstration of eclecticism that his clients may not have expected and he did not intend.

Thom had discovered a landscape gardener and nurseryman, Raoul Robillard, who was uniquely attuned to his own views about siting and plant materials in the Vancouver climate, and he built in a sub-contract for him in almost every project. As a result, Thom's houses of this period have a remarkable and recognizable consistency of expression, even though they respond fully to different programs, siting conditions, size requirements and budgets, and even though they were not all designed using the same formal vocabulary.

Works/Baker house

Figure 30
This medium-size house with its thin flat roof, its south-facing living room glass wall and the generous overhang clearly illustrates the elements of Thom's evolving formal language in the mid-1950s. The raised section of the roof is a 1982 addition designed by Thom.

Moult house

Figure 31
The south-facing deck overlooking Burrard Inlet and Stanley Park. The fascia board on the edge of the roof and the slotted recessed decoration under it, is a reproduction of a Frank Lloyd Wright detail, probably from the Melvin Maxwell Smith house, 1946, in Bloomfield Hills, Michigan.

31

32

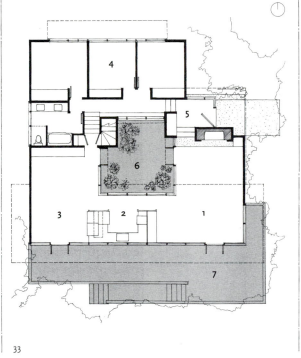

33

Moult house

Figure 32
The enclosed court from the
living room.

Figure 33
The plan.
1 *living room/library*
2 *kitchen*
3 *family room*
4 *bedrooms*
5 *entry*
6 *court*
7 *deck*

Figure 34
The living room.

34

Dodek house

Figure 35
The living room. The Dodeks became close friends of Ron and he was a recurrent visitor throughout his career. The corner near the Japanese print was one of his favourite hideaways.

Figure 36
The garden court as seen from the interior corridor in this 1958 picture, is now dominated by the wisteria vine, seen here on the post, that now surrounds the whole court at window-head level.

38

37

Ames house

Figure 37
A street-level view of this large family house showing the continuous strip window under the eaves, which lights the bedrooms and the stairwell. Note how the sill follows the slope of the roof.

Figure 38
The living room and the master bedroom over it, both overlook the patio and swimming pool and the dense planting screen, to the left in the picture, giving privacy from the street.

Rogers/Dumaresq house

Figure 39
A very large multi-level house on a steep site, as partly seen from the swimming pool.

39

42

Rogers/Dumaresq house

Figure 40
The patio entrance to the two-storey living room.

Figure 41
The dining room on the second floor. The sloping section of the roof gives it an intimate scale and quality, and the strip windows provide panoramic views of the gardens.

Figure 42
The approach to the living room from the entrance area, which is on a level between the main floor and the second floor.

41

43

Termuende house

Figure 43
The living room with stone fireplace, wall and columns.

Figure 44
This additional wing built on an existing house provided the new living room, bedrooms and a business office for the owner. The space of the lower floor living room and the swimming pool were literally blasted out of the rock site, and the granite stones obtained were used for the structure of the building and the terracing around the pool.

Figure 45
The sun terrace overlooking the view and pool.

44

45

Narod house

Figure 46
This remarkable house came about from a challenge by close friends of Thom, an engineer and his wife, who had already bought a small left-over piece of property on the waterfront and developed a conceptual design for the structure, but were not certain about the next steps. The upper deck is at street level on one side, and on the other side, is cantilevered over the water to get spectacular views of the harbour and mountains. What appears to be separate sections of deck are in fact continuous across the whole side of the building.

48

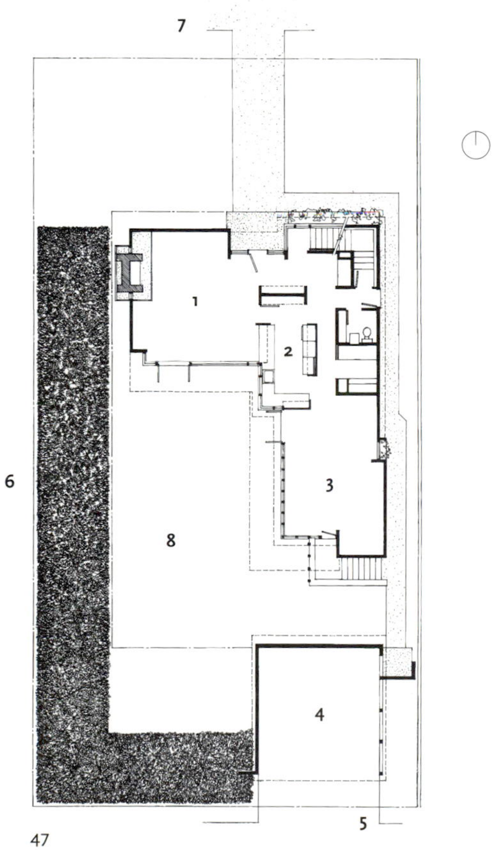

Rogaway/Segal house

Figure 47
This house is a prototypical family house for a large suburban corner lot. Thom used variations of this plan many times. The novel feature is the calculated distribution of sections of the house around the perimeter of the allowed building area on the lot, and the use of high (fifteen feet plus) and dense plant material to fill in the remainder of the perimeter to guarantee privacy and reduce street noises, while, at the same time providing an inner court. In this plan, the L-shaped gray area designates the planting area, which could be a trimmed hedge of laurel or cedar, or mixed trees and shrubs depending on the surrounding situation.

1 *living/dining room*
2 *kitchen*
3 *family room*
4 *carport*
5 *lane*
6 *minor street and sidewalk*
7 *major street*
8 *court*

Figure 48
The garden court, large enough for a children's playground as well as a more formal patio off the living room.

47

8 Massey College

IN 1960 RON THOM RECEIVED a personal invitation from Vincent Massey, on behalf of the Massey Foundation, to participate in a limited design competition to select an architect and a design for a building at the University of Toronto to be called Massey College. This was a highly prestigious project to be built at Canada's largest university, for a distinguished and knowledgeable client. It would be the first potential commission for a large project Thom would bring into Thompson, Berwick, Pratt on his own account. In hindsight, it was the most catalytic event of his career.

Massey College, completed in 1963, is the most recent project initiated and built by the Massey Foundation. Earlier buildings on the University of Toronto campus built by the Massey family in this century include that for the Lillian Massey School of Household Science, built in 1906, and Hart House, the student union, started in 1911 and completed in 1919. Prior to that, the Massey family was well known for other major benefactions, particularly in the humanities. Probably the best known of these is Massey Hall in Toronto, which was, and still is, a favourite site for important musical and other cultural events, some of which were also supported by the Massey Foundation.

Vincent Massey, as a young man, had been intimately involved with the architects in the detailed development of Hart House from inception to its opening, and he had revealed a considerable knowledge and understanding of architecture.[1] As well, according to Claude Bissell, *Vincent had emerged as an important young man in the community—affluent, talented, with interests that embraced education, politics, and the arts. Hart House was an institution that embraced all three, and he could use it to advance the cause of each.*[2]

Through his interests in the theatre, he was instrumental in the creation of the Hart House Theatre.

He, and his wife also, had an interest in music, and this led to the formation of the Hart House String Quartet which, with the support of the Massey Foundation, went on to achieve international recognition. Some time later, Vincent, as chairman of the Foundation, went on to add to this record. The Massey Medal Awards program in architecture, in operation from 1951 to 1970, was a particular stimulus to Ron Thom as well as other architects of his generation.

As Vincent Massey's term as Governor General of Canada was coming to an end, the early discussions took place about a new project the Foundation might undertake at the University of Toronto. Ideas coalesced into a proposal for a graduate residence. In his memoir, Massey states that on December 1959 he wrote a letter to the Chairman of the Board of Governors and to the President of the University in which he described the project as follows: *The project we have in mind is prompted by the growing importance of the body of graduate students of the University, and we have been considering what might be done to give them fitting living accommodation and a sense of their common purpose and responsibilities which, by their advanced work, will rest upon them. We have come to the conclusion that our object can best be achieved by the establishment of an institution whose membership would be drawn from those graduate students of special promise, and that its organization—we would call it a college—should be such as to minister to the life of its members in every way. The number of students housed would necessarily be limited and we are of the view that the institution should be for men. We are encouraged by the distinguished part which has been played by certain collegiate establishments for graduate students in English and American universities, and we are convinced that the influence of an institution such as we have in mind would be highly beneficial in the University of Toronto . . . the object of the Foundation,*

Figure 49
The entrance from
Devonshire Place.

in proposing to erect the building, is to provide an institution for graduate students of the greatest promise, and that the College (to be called Massey College) should represent quality in every aspect. The purpose of the institution would not be to simply house a group of graduate students, but to select the best men available and to form a distinguished collegiate community.[3]

Five days later the University formally accepted the gift, calling it "an imaginative acquisition that would never have been financed by the state or by a public appeal."[4]

At that time the Trustees of the Foundation were Vincent Massey (chairman), his sons Lionel and Hart, his brother Raymond, Raymond's son Geoffrey and Wilmot Broughall, an officer of the National Trust Company who looked after the Foundation's financial affairs. Raymond Massey was not able to attend any of the proposed meetings, and so did not participate in the development of the project. Both Hart and Geoff Massey are architects, who were then practising in Ottawa and Vancouver, respectively. The subject of the appointment of an architect was one that surfaced early. As architects themselves, the two younger trustees became strong advocates for giving the opportunity to an up-and-coming modernist. Vincent wrote: *it was impossible for the six trustees to agree on the choice of an architect: the best plan seemed to be to select a small group of architects and write them to submit diagrams and models from which we could make a choice.*[5]

The trustees finally agreed to hold a limited design competition by invitation to select the architect and the design for Massey College.[6]

Vincent Massey started to put on paper the detailed space requirements, including descriptions of how the various components were to interrelate and be used. Hart was put to work on site studies, including rough bulk-form analyses to determine

the approximate size and possible configurations of the project, and to assist Vincent and the others in the client group to understand the problems which would be presented by the various sites available on the campus, so that they could make the best choice. Later, he put together a final document that was given to the competitors as a basis from which to develop a design. Even at this early stage, Vincent was adamant that the building should be built around a quadrangle which would be a private space for the use of the residents for College activities only. His models for his vision of the college were All Souls and Balliol Colleges at Oxford, which were familiar to him from his student days there. These spaces, with their enclosed courts and precincts, had the quality and ambience which characterized for him the Oxford experience. Hart and Lionel, who had also been students there, and the others agreed with this vision. Coupled with other site features, this set very specific constraints on the design problem. In the memorandum attached to the letter of invitation the vision was presented simply by the statement "it is our wish that the building should be in quadrangular form," but that document also includes a paragraph outlining their more programmatic and qualitative aspirations for the college: *Massey College as a college for graduate students will be unique in Canada. There is nothing comparable to it in any Canadian university. It is of great importance that it should, in its form, reflect the life that goes on inside it, and should possess certain qualities—dignity, grace, beauty and warmth. Such a college as we have in mind possesses antecedents in various countries, and whatever their physical forms may be or the date of their erection, they have a character in common. What we wish is a home for a community of scholars whose life will have intimacy but at the same time, academic dignity.*[7]

After considering several sites, the trustees and

the University agreed on a fine site at the corner of Hoskin Avenue and Devonshire Place, adjacent to St. Hilda's College on the north along Devonshire Place, near Trinity College to the east, and across Hoskin Avenue from the central campus within view of Hart House to the south. The site was then formally deeded to the College.

The remaining task was to develop a list of architects who would participate in the competition. The two architect-trustees were assigned to the task. Geoff recommended Vancouver architects Arthur Erickson and Ron Thom. Hart recommended Carmen Corneil and John Parkin from Toronto. The trustees agreed and the competition got underway.

Vincent Massey sent a letter to the four competitors on February 4, 1960, inviting each to 'submit preliminary design drawings' for the project, enclosing the memorandum which outlined the decisions taken by the trustees to that date, The letter included a description of the project in the briefest of terms and a statement that the fee payable for their participation would be $3000 each. It also included an invitation to come to "Batterwood," Vincent's country home near Port Hope, Ontario, for the day with the other candidates to meet the trustees for a discussion and briefing session, to be followed by a dinner.

The significance of this invitation to these young architects, each at the early stage of his career, cannot be underestimated. It presented an opportunity to the winner of the competition to design and build a major building (nearly $2 million, including furnishing, in 1960) in Toronto at a major university. It was also a chance to work for a highly prestigious group of clients who were sensitive to both modern and traditional ideas in architecture and to the importance of the architect's role. And, they were insisting on high quality in all aspects of the enterprise to develop a unique project which was to be at the same time

experimental, controversial and highly visible.

For Ron Thom, a new partner in TBP for little over a year and anxious to confirm that the confidence the Vancouver firm had shown in him was justified, the letter of invitation from Vincent Massey came at just the right time. He knew he was going to be up against some tough competition, but he was ready and eager for it. Parkin was the same age as Thom, but was already well-known for his commitment to modern architecture and the high quality of his design work, backed up by the rapidly growing strength of the office he and his partners had created. Carmen Corneil was unknown to Thom. Another contemporary, he was a prize winning graduate of the University of Toronto with a modest practice in Toronto, who had just returned from two years in Norway and Finland and work with Alvar Aalto. At that time Thom saw Erickson, whom he new well, as an enigmatic competitor of his own age just starting in practise on his own turf, but he treated him with respect. Erickson, too, must have seen Vincent's letter with some relish. Teaching at the University of B.C. to make ends meet, and starting an office on his own, he needed a high-profile project to make his name. If he won, it would be his first major commission. He was confident he had, because of his recent travels, more first-hand knowledge of the 'Oxbridge' college precedents than any of the other competitors, and therefore understood the nuances of the project better.

The meeting of the participants with Vincent and Lionel Massey took place at Batterwood on February 15. This occasion was Vincent's solution to his concern that *none of the candidates had any experience of college life, and it was obviously necessary to convey to these young men what a college really was. Without understanding the conception, they could hardly be expected to prepare a building in which Massey College could be housed . . .We stipulated that it should be in the form of a quadrangle—that it should be turned inwards, not outwards, excluding the turmoil and clamour of the modern city, and giving its residents the quiet and peace in which an academic community should appropriately live.*[8]

The candidates returned to their offices with the detailed program in their hands and a due date of June 30 for their presentation drawings.

On that date, five of the trustees assembled at Batterwood for a long day of jury duty, arguing the pros and cons of the four schemes submitted in Round 1. These clearly reflected the level of understanding and the attitude of each of the competitors to the college as proposed by the trustees. Bissell, in his imaginative account of these events, suggests that *The jury's decision would rest mainly on the architects' success in embodying the concept of the College: a community of scholars concerned with the inner life of the mind, but not cut off from the outside world; a constant reminder, particularly in the communal areas, that beauty and truth were intertwined.*[9]

Parkin produced a classic modernist solution organized on two axes, with a perfectly rationalized structure and plan. According to the jury, "it was evident that very considerable effort went into the work . . . however, it [met a] consensus of opinion that [his] design did not reflect the spirit of the College as they conceived it."[10] From the photographs of the model, the building appears curiously overscaled in its surroundings—because of its relentless symmetry it needed a larger site and free space all around it to give it an appropriate setting.

At this distance in time, of the four schemes, Erickson's looks to be the most promising, although it needed simplification and further development. It, too, demonstrated an uncompromising Modernist approach, and a reluctance to respond literally to the directive of the enclosed quadrangle. Both Parkin's

and Erickson's schemes were quite open to access from the surrounding streets, but their quads had a private feeling to them. Corneil openly defied the intent of the inward-looking closed quad that had been requested, and argued in an explanatory note, that "by leaving a third of the long side on Devonshire Place open to all, [he was] establishing visual ties with the skyline and towers of University College, while providing the benefit of spaciousness in the quadrangle and added visual importance for the hall."[11] He, too, had convictions, and they were in conflict with those of the trustees.

Ron Thom took the program literally, and his plan shows a perimeter building forming a completely private quadrangle, with the one access from the side street controlled by a gate and a porter's lodge. The communal spaces were clustered at the south end, and they thrust into the quad along the central long axis. The plan form and massing are reminiscent of Frank Lloyd Wright's Imperial Hotel in Tokyo. The big volume spaces of the major rooms were grouped within this central building and given a massive, multi-layered hip roof with soaring overhangs, a carryover from his own experience with large houses. In addition, the central building and the doorways to the five "houses" around the quad were heavily ornamented. This prompted the Trustees to comment that "the general treatment and ornamentation has produced a character that is considered inappropriate to a College of this nature in this environment, in this age [more reminiscent of the] orient, early 20th century, Wright, [there is] the danger of such a building becoming dated."[12]

At the end of the day the trustees had reached a consensus that Parkin's design was the least interesting. In addition, they agreed that of the other three, none was clearly a winner and that all three needed more work to enable the trustees to decide

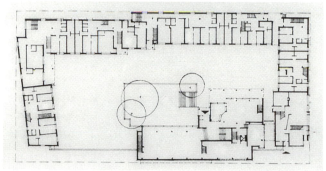

50

Round 1, First floor plans as submitted.

Figure 50
John Parkin

Figure 51
Carmen Corneil

Figure 52
Arthur Erickson

Figure 53
Ron Thom

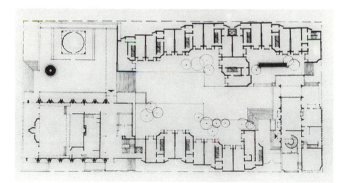

51

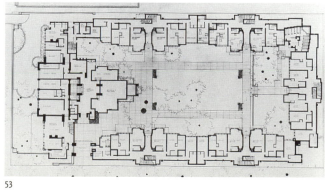

52

53

Round 1, Presentation drawings,
watercolours by Ron Thom

Figure 54
Dining Hall on the upper floor
on the Hoskin Avenue elevation.

Figure 55
View into the quadrangle on
entry into the college.

Figure 56
View in the quadrangle, looking
back left to the entrance, and
straight ahead to the common
rooms with the Dining Hall in
the background.

54

55

Figure 57
Pencil drawing by Ron Thom:
a freehand sectional elevation,
a preliminary study of the central building.

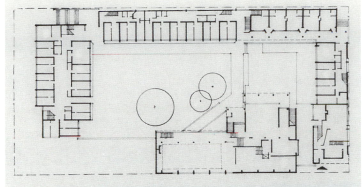

58

finally on one or the other. Accordingly, they then summarized their critiques of each scheme in point-form notes under the headings 'Impressions' and 'Planning'. The notes were explicit regarding the closure of the quadrangle in both Erickson's and Corneil's schemes. Subsequently, letters were sent conveying these decisions to the candidates. Parkin was not invited to continue. The others received an invitation along with the trustees' critique and their requirements for the next presentation, which set the date of October 15 for the final decision. An additional fee of $1500 each was approved for Round 2.[13] All three architects agreed to continue under these terms.

On the prescribed date, the five trustees assembled again, this time to jury the Round 2 presentations which were more elaborate and included new, more finished models and more comprehensive drawings, including perspective drawings of the interiors of specific rooms. Thom's scheme, the non-residential parts of which had gone through an extensive reorganization in plan and elevation, and a change of character, had the impact of an entirely new scheme. It emerged the winner by a unanimous decision of the trustees.

Both Erickson's and Corneil's final schemes clearly showed a reluctance to make changes other than those insisted upon by the written critique they had received, and then not all of them. Neither had changed the character of the building, and they remained strong modernist statements. Corneil's scheme was particularly austere, judging from the photos of the presentation, yet from the written statement he provided in Round 1, one conjures up a beautiful light-filled environment, student rooms with wall-to-wall horizontal windows, and daylit communal rooms as "white spaces set off by warm materials—copper, tile, and wood."[14] The jury, how-

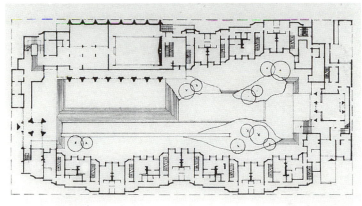

59

60

Round 2, First floor plans

Figure 58
Carmen Corneil

Figure 59
Arthur Erickson

Figure 60
Ron Thom

61

ever, found it to be "very restrained almost to the point of dullness." While he did ask for and had a supplementary meeting [15] with some of the trustees in Toronto to discuss their written comments on his Round 1 submission, his final scheme failed to change their minds.

As Thom developed his Round 2 submission and revised the plan and form of the building to respond to the clients' comments, he removed the pitched roofs. Suddenly, he must have seen the whole complex as one building, and, at that moment, he found his form. In an article on the competition in *Canadian Architect* he is quoted as saying: . . . *a limited architectural vocabulary has been deliberately made common to the building as a whole and individual parts are expressed within this vocabulary. The total concept is of a quadrangle, secluded on four sides by the building from the outside noise and confusion, acting as a court-yard common room.* [16] The various parts of the complex were then identified by the careful articulation of their mass, height and silhouette, walls, the doors, entrances, and the windows within a very limited range of materials. The interiors were developed as an extension of the same vocabulary with the addition of a few new materials to add close-up colour and textures at the point of touch contact. The grid-like patterning of the window mullions of the major components and their extension above the roof produce a silhouette and character vaguely reminiscent of Gothic details, yet it is achieved with simple means. With this vocabulary firmly in his mind, Thom's natural genius for composition came into play, and the result is harmonious and serene.

Ron Thom's Round 2 design was clearly the most highly developed and the most convincing submission. The trustees, considering their program, were unanimous in their enthusiasm for his solution, which met all of their conditions and hopes for the College.

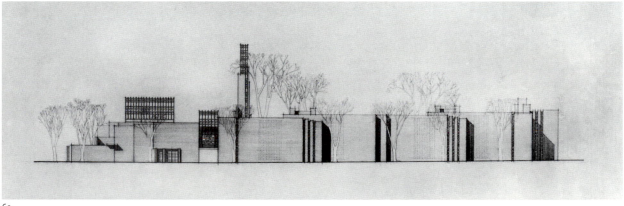

62

Round 2, Model and presentation drawings by Ron Thom

Figure 61
Aerial view of the model.

Figure 62
Street elevations.

63

64

Pencil renderings by
Barry Downs:

Figure 63
The College as seen at the
corner of Hoskin Avenue and
Devonshire Place

Figure 64
The Quadrangle

Figure 65
The Dining Hall

65

FOLLOWING ON THE SIGNING of a contract with Thompson, Berwick, Pratt of Vancouver, naming Ron Thom as 'partner-in-charge,' the project moved into the developmental design stage. Thom arrived in his new capacity for his first business meeting with the Foundation, confident but still slightly in awe of Vincent Massey. However, this feeling was soon overcome as they both became engaged in the detailed development of the project. A mutual respect quickly developed as work progressed.

During the preparation of the building contract drawings and other documents, Thom became intimately involved in resolving the detailing of every aspect of the building. In order to speed up the construction process, it is not unusual to defer the final design of whole components that will be installed after the major elements of the building enclosure are in place, as well as the choice of the sub-contractors for those components. Cost allowances for them are included as part of the general contract. During the first phase of construction, the architect develops the details for that component, and bids are obtained from appropriate subcontractors. After his selection, "shop drawings" are then made by the sub-contractor working on-site in consultation with the architect and the general contractor, and the final prices are established at that time. Thom loved this part of the process, as it is the point at which the architect has the final decision, and it is a test of his control of the project to see if he could get all the exact detail he wants, and deliver a saving to his client or an improved detail within the established budget framework. The feeling of power is exhilarating, and this was the first major commission for which Thom had had this measure of control.

What is remarkable is that much of the ornamentation that Thom had removed from his Round 1 submission, to achieve the simplicity and clarity in his winning scheme in Round 2, comes back in the building as built, albeit in a more appropriate form. That it does attests to the tenacity with which Thom pursued his ideas and also his ability to find a way to make them happen. As well, it speaks of his ability to bring the client along to both accept the changes and to pay for the difference in cost, if that was required.

An opportunity for some cost saving appears to have occurred in the bidding process for the pre-cast window frames. These are shown on the detailed tender drawings dated October 1961 as being made of pre-cast reinforced concrete, and the decorative pinnacle caps are shown on the vertical mullions as separate concrete components. The final details as-built are shown on the shop drawings of the winning bidder, Ritchie Stone Co., as being made of limestone, and the spandrel panels have decorative designs cast into them which were not on the first drawings, but were affordable even within the low bid.[17] Still further embellishment included the addition of decorative metal screens in the gates and above the parapet of the Porter's Lodge, and in the open corners of the brick fence of the Master's Lodge. These metalwork items are true 'extras' to the total contract, probably added to solve problems of security that were not readily apparent earlier. The overall effect of this and other enrichment is to give the building an affinity with the older colleges on the campus, which are designed in traditional styles, but it stops short of conformity to those styles. At the same time, the simplicity of the main elements and the planar composition of the bell tower clearly reveal Thom's modernist leanings.

Hart and Geoff Massey, with the addition of the newly appointed Master-Designate Robertson Davies, were all involved with Vincent Massey and Ron Thom for specific matters as the building became more finite, deciding on details of plan or furnishing, all of which involved considerable letter writing and plan checking to a tight schedule. By this time Thom had demonstrated his great facility and competence with the design of the interior detailing of the building, and his contract was extended to include the design of built-in cabinetry, bookcases, lighting fixtures, special chairs and other furniture, and to select the draperies, and carpets, and the other furniture and furnishings. [In the design of at least one chair, he proved himself to be the equal of his mentor, Frank Lloyd Wright, who achieved international distinction for designing and building some of the world's most uncomfortable chairs, however elegant and appropriate they seem to be.][18] His mandate included the selection and coordination of other designers and craftsmen to design and develop particular items. They included: Alan Fleming and Debbie Adams, from Toronto (lettering); Ed Drahanchuck, from Alberta (pottery); Eric Clements, Birmingham, England (silverware) and Tanya Moiseiwitsch (the chapel interior). From all accounts, Thom reached a pinnacle of his capabilities for team leadership in design production during this phase of the project.

In parallel, the planning and implementation of the governing structure and administrative arrangements for the College were developing under the direction of the new Master, Robertson Davies. Claude Bissell, in his biography of Vincent Massey, comments on this stage: *Davies entered upon his administrative duties with enthusiasm and vigour. There were numerous theoretical matters about the government of the college to be settled. The first meeting of the Master and Fellows took place on 24 November 1961 in the Senate Room of the main administrative building of the university, Simcoe Hall, and Massey commented that 'one felt that the college had really come into being.*

There were also continuous and passionate meetings about every detail of the college furnishings. Vincent saw in the college a chance to implement fully his conviction that the physical surroundings have a profound effect on attitudes and manners. Massey College was to be the complete embodiment of his aesthetic faith. Colour and form were to spell out an attitude towards life. This must not be confused with luxury, Massey pointed out, which was often vulgar and ostentatious. He was irritated when much was made of the invitation to twenty of the world's leading silver designers to design the college silver. The winning design by Eric Clements of Birmingham, England, he pointed out, 'was one of extreme simplicity.'[19]

In May, Thom was caught up in Vincent Massey's arrangements for the laying of the cornerstone, his first taste of pomp and ceremony. The event had been arranged to coincide with a visit of Prince Philip to Canada to attend a conference on industrial problems in the Commonwealth. The dignitaries in attendance were included in the invitation, so that the event turned into a grand occasion with a distinct international flavour, amplified by a trumpet fanfare provided by four military bandsmen in full regalia.

The building was completed on schedule in the spring of 1963, and the official opening took place in October. The main event was a private dinner at which Vincent Massey and his guests hosted the first group of junior fellows and the full complement of senior fellows, another memorable occasion, according to Claude Bissell.[20]

Figure 66
The quadrangle looking toward the bell tower and the common room with the Dining Hall above, and the residences to the left.

Figure 67
A walking view of the quadrangle.

67

Figure 68
The Hoskin Avenue front,
facing the university.

Figure 69
The Round Room, used for
special occasions, discussions
with visitors, thesis examinations, etc.

69

Figure 70
The north end of the quadrangle. The chapel entrance can
be seen in the left corner
between the two walls, marked
by its thin canopy roof and
short spire structure.

Figure 71
The long wall on Devonshire
Place. The slot windows provide light for the back access
corridor to the stairs and to
individual rooms.

71

The official opening and the ceremonies signalled a high-point in Ron Thom's career. He had had a classic relationship with a client under near-perfect circumstances, particularly during the last year of construction and fitting out of the building. He had been involved in every detail as he worked with admiring and highly creative craftsmen on furnishings, cabinetry, furniture, lighting and tableware. He had been on-site away from his partners for long periods dealing with all aspects of this one job directly with Vincent Massey, the principal client/patron. Vincent was completely at home in this role, re-living his experience at Hart House, working one-on-one with his architect. Understanding the process and able to give the project almost full-time attention, he demanded quality, but he was open to and encouraged this young architect. Everything about this experience further strengthened Thom's conviction that this was the only way to make architecture.

THE COLLEGE HAS BEEN IN USE now for more than thirty years, and remains in remarkably good shape. Ultimately, this can only be attributed to an institution which takes pride in and looks after its property. The viability of the concept and the design of the building, as well as the sense of community, have been fostered and maintained by successive masters and the governing body of senior fellows. Probably the most severe test of the concept and the design came with a fundamental change in the admissions policy to admit women as Junior and Senior Fellows in 1973. Surprisingly, this was accomplished with no physical changes to the building. One senior fellow attributes this to "the extravagant number of 3-piece conventional bathrooms provided in the original design which has made the Fellows' rooms interchangeable and functional for both men and women. Sharing a bathroom here with only two or three others is no different from the situation in a family at home."[21] With the current mix of junior fellows being equally men and women (coincidentally, not as the result of a quota) and a more or less random assignment of rooms, there appear to be no serious problems or complaints.

The current Master, Anne Saddlemeyer, says that "the sense of community has improved with the change." There is no doubt that both the donors' conviction regarding the strength of the "college" idea, and the student selection method, have been tested and vindicated. The donors' ability to articulate their vision in great detail captured Ron Thom's imagination and inspired his sensitive interpretation of it. The resulting building feels right and appropriate for all of its various functions. As the British-Canadian architectural critic Peter Collins wrote in the *Manchester Guardian* just after the building was finished: "the Massey Foundation asked for a building that would be eminently functional, eminently sturdy, and eminently beautiful, and that is what they got."[22]

ARTHUR ERICKSON, discussing the competition for Massey College in an interview over thirty years after the event, pointed out that "there is a remarkable similarity between my Round 1 plan of the quadrangle and Ron's final plan. On the way home to Vancouver from the Batterwood briefing, Ron and I made a pact that we would show each other our schemes at the end of Round 1, before we sent them to the Jury." At that time they did not know there would be a second Round. When that did occur and Erickson saw the results, he says he was surprised to see that "Ron copied my plan, i.e., the concept, but brought his sensibility to it."[23]

The word "copying" is pejorative, at least to some

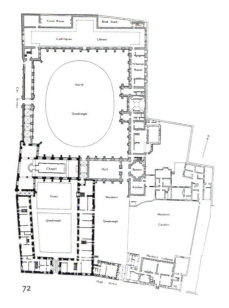

72

Figure 72
All Souls College, Oxford
University.

Figure 73
The Imperial Hotel, Tokyo, by
Frank Lloyd Wright.

Figure 74
Thom's Round 1 plan
(redrawn).

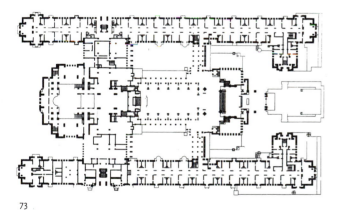

73

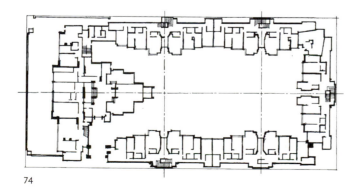

74

of us, although not to Ron Thom, as can be seen in the quotation in the previous chapter from an article where he was writing about about how we learn to design, "we all begin via the process of eclecticism . . . this is a natural and proper phase in the learning process. Every child learns by imitation." On the assumption that Thom would not be offended by the remark, it seems appropriate to test Erickson's claim by examining the principal design decisions Thom must have gone through, based on the evidence available, to develop his Round 2 submission which won him the contract to build it. The sequence would have been as follows.

- On his arrival in Toronto for the briefing by Vincent Massey, he toured the site, its surrounding buildings, the landscaping, and its position with respect to the university.

- He travelled back to Vancouver with Arthur Erickson after the briefing and talked about Vincent's ideas about and concept for this project, as well as about the Oxbridge precedents that Erickson new at first hand, but which Thom had never seen.

- Once home, he read the programmatic material which outlined details of the site and the required accommodation, and proceeded to categorize the functional components and their functional relationships. This would lead to a very preliminary analysis of the site and some diagramming to explore alternative positioning of these functional components.

- He sought inspirational precedents to get clues as to the appropriate scale, character, space, materials, light, and expression of such a building. He would have examined books on the Oxford colleges, and read some of their history. In searching for a more contemporary example he thought of the Imperial Hotel in Tokyo by Frank Lloyd Wright, which has similar functional components, and became interested in its planning and residential character.

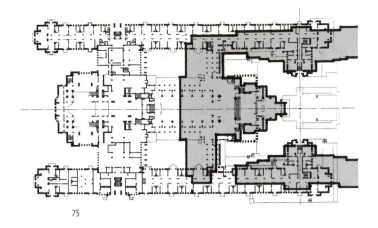

75

82

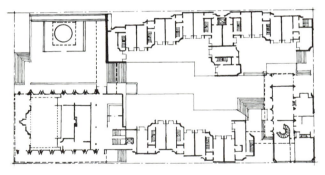

76

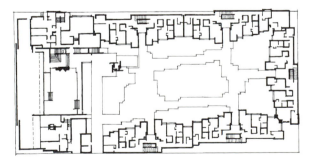

77

• He started to develop his own plan in detail, arranging the residential accomodation in five "houses," each serviced by two stairs, a vertical unit three stories high, housing about twenty students. The library, common room, and the dining room and its service functions were all integrated into a single block at one end of the site, and the houses were placed two on each side, and one across the open end, thus surrounding a large quadrangular space. The plan is symmetrical about the long axis. The more he worked on this scheme, the more it took on features of the Imperial Hotel, particularly the hip-roofed central block as seen only from the quadrangle, the character of many of Wright's large houses, and even its proportions in plan. His presentation drawings show the highly decorated windows of the highest space, the dining room.

Just before they mailed off their entries, Erickson and Thom met to show each other their proposals, thinking this was the end of the process. As we know, the foundation was not satisfied with the results, and the competition went another round from which Thom emerged the winner. It is at this point that we can pose the question: "Is there any noticeable change we can find in Thom's Round 2 final plan that can be attributed to his seeing Erickson's Round 1 plan?" If there is anything to consider, it lies in the plan configuration and detail, in particular that of the external wall of the student rooms facing and surrounding the quadrangle in each of these two proposals.

The walls in Erickson's first proposal are given an ordered and rhythmic effect by making all the rooms the same width and grouping them in stacked pairs spaced by narrower stair corridors on each side. These vertical clusters are then placed in rows so that their open faces form a stepped wall. Each room's face onto the quad is recessed between its sidewalls, and a bay window is placed there to bring the central area of that face out to the plane of the end of the side walls. The total effect would be a rich and changing three-dimensional patterning of light, shade, transparencies and reflections.

Thom, rescued from his obsessive Wrightian roofs and decorations by the jury in Round 1, stripped them all off in his Round 2 proposal, threw away the axis of symmetry and concentrated on replanning, in particular, the major rooms at the south end of the site. The result was a completely unified scheme, all parts connected, wth a single vocabulary. In the process, his housing units did not change very much in their internal plan configuration, but they had to be shifted slightly out of their former symmetrical alignment to accommodate changes in the size and placement of the larger rooms. As a result, the plan of the quadrangle is slightly skewed into a looser configuration. The wall formed by the houses on the quad is almost identical to his first proposal in plan, a stepped surface of vertical panels of brick and glass. By setting some whole houses back or forward in their alignment, the wall becomes more continuous, and the houses are not so clearly delineated. While the wall that results may suggest some similarity to Erickson's proposal in plan, in fact, the differences in the window treatment in the two architects' proposals make this discussion academic, if not irrelevant.

Arising directly out of the decisions they had taken by presenting the proposals they did in Round 1, both contestants had valid reasons of their own to continue to develop them according to their own sensitivity, and they did just that. What this exercise demonstrates is that Ron, at this stage of his development, used precedent where he could find it, and was a quick learner, able to find the principle and synthesize it into a new context to meet specifically different requirements. The end product may be eclectic, but it is also original.

ON COMPLETION, Massey College came in for immediate criticism for its supposedly 'elitist style' and 'Oxbridge manners', and its 'men only' focus, all of which was capably and eloquently dealt with by the Master, Robertson Davies. The architectural magazines' critics were divided in their appraisal of it as a modernist building, or as some hybrid that would set architecture back fifty years. In 1993, Brigitte Shim, in a short article in the Anniversary Edition of 'The Massey Bull," an in-house College paper, gives her opinion on this subject, which provides a unifying view: *Has Massey College set Canadian architecture back fifty years as one critic suggested at its opening? In 1963, Massey College challenged the modern architectural concepts expressed in the leading architectural magazines in Europe and North America. The College, deliberately built with brick and limestone instead of glass curtain wall, was criticized as old fashioned and unreflective of contemporary technology.*

Thirty years later, it can be said that Massey College is both modern and traditional, institutional and domestic, monumental and intimate. These complex and often contradictory characteristics are the architect's response to Vincent Massey's programme for the College . . .

Ron Thom designed a total environment at Massey College including the building, its landscape, its interior fittings. He promoted collaboration with stone carvers, calligraphers, silversmiths, and potters to create a work which is a full expression of life.

While describing his views on the expression of architecture, Thom stated; "architecture, at its best, still has the inherent power to celebrate the human functions it accommodates and there is nothing to suggest

Figure 75
The Imperial Hotel with Thom's Round 1 plan superimposed.

Figure 76
Erickson's Round 1 plan (redrawn).

Figure 77
Thom's Round 2 plan (redrawn).

that the new constraints that may come should impede the ability of architecture to extend and enrich life in our society."

Massey College continues to extend and enrich lives and has come to be appreciated as a significant building in Canadian architecture.

In response to the critics of 1963 and their dogmatic views, I believe that Massey College defines a rich alternative modern tradition—one with roots in the past as well as its contemporary condition and one that can guide us into the future.[24]

As 1963 APPROACHED, Thom was facing some major decisions with respect to his own future. He had met and fallen in love with Molly Golby, with whom he was working on Massey College—she was the research assistant to Allan Fleming, the consultant for graphics and industrial design. Thom had also just received an invitation to make a submission on behalf of his firm to the committee selecting an architect for the planning and design of Trent University. Things were definitely looking promising in Toronto, and he was starting to assess the possibilities of starting a new life and practice there.

9 Trent University

ONE OF THE PREDICTABLE OUTCOMES of the baby boom was the inevitable arrival of a large portion of this generation onto the doorsteps of the universities, beginning in earnest in the 1960s. By the time they actually arrived the so-called "knowledge explosion" had already made its impact upon the existing institutions, and all signs pointed to the continuous expansion and importance of this phenomenon. One major consequence was the demand for new kinds of facilities to accommodate the rising enrolments and increasing research interests. The multiplication of new disciplines arising from new areas of specialized knowledge resulted in new job creation and therefore a rising rate of participation in university-level education.

Expansion required at the predicted rate of growth in Ontario could only be resolved by a combination of rapid construction of new facilities at the existing "big five" universities and by the construction of new universities. Serious consideration had to be given to curricula, new teaching faculty resources and their location and recruitment, and the development of appropriate planning and administrative structures within government and the institutions. Several of the big universities were landlocked in burgeoning urban areas, and demographic studies were showing a dispersal of students across the province. The practical realities of trading-off land acquisition, infrastructure and construction costs in dense urban areas against lower costs in smaller towns soon became apparent and politically attractive. By a mixture of options, Ontario chose to renovate and make major additions to its established universities, as well as adding nine new universities to make a total of fourteen in the province, dispersed regionally.

Time was the enemy. Even with the best skills of the demographers, as everything was in a state of change at once, accurate predictions as to where and how many of these students were going to arrive at a given university were rare. The responsible provincial government ministry which had to find the locations, the land and the planners, create the new institutions, set the standards for both the education and the buildings, allocate the capital and operating funds available and dole it out equitably, had to do so in competition with the equally pressing demands of all the other public service sectors. To assist in this enterprise and to protect their own interests, the existing universities in Ontario formed their own Council of Ontario Universities, adding new member universities as soon as the ink on their charters was dry. The Ministry of Education set up an Advisory Committee on University Affairs to do the research to develop policy, priorities, standards and formulae for funding and space allocation, and so on. These two bodies in collaboration established the basis for negotiations between the universities and the government.

The new universities soon found themselves toeing the line within a defined framework for higher education built on the model of the existing big-five universities, and playing a game of catch-up. This was, of course, necessary, but by its very nature, it presented a formidable challenge requiring both experimentation and innovation. The flow of the postwar generation through the university system was predictable and finite, but the danger was that the new universities may not be firmly enough established to be viable when the flow decreased significantly. As it happened, the flow of capital funding from government was stopped in the late 1970s and did not resume again significantly except for designated projects with matching funding from other sources. It is against this background of a rapidly decreasing budget, and hence the necessity to get as much completely built, equipped and staffed as possible before the money dried up, that one has to look at Trent University and Ron Thom's involvement with it.

NEW UNIVERSITIES get started in many different ways, as a direct response to government policies, as the result of philanthropy and sometimes by the happy coincidence of tenacious civic action, academic vision and philanthropy. Of the nine new universities built in Ontario, Trent University is a remarkable example of this last option.

A group of six prominent citizen-activists in the town of Peterborough had been formed in the mid-1950s as a Planning Committee to study the feasibility of establishing a junior college there, for which there was wide popular support. After a number of exploratory meetings, their sights had been raised to seek to establish a provincial university, and, in 1960 "the 'Mayor's Committee' became the 'Trent College Board of Directors . . . The Board set itself various tasks: the selection of a President; the location of a temporary home for the first teaching years, as well as a permanent site; the wooing of the provincial government; and the planning of a founding fund-raising drive."[1] As a first step and after a short search, the board appointed Professor Thomas Symons (then Dean of Devonshire House at the University of Toronto) as their choice for president, and in the interim, as academic consultant and chairman of the academic planning committee, and as president designate.[2]

In 1962 the Premier of Ontario, John Robarts, agreed to support the granting of a charter, and Trent University came into being in the spring of 1963. Its charter specified that the university would be governed by a Senate and a Board of Governors. The original six governors were named in the charter, and they consisted of five of the original Peterborough founders and Professor Symons, who was also appointed as president. The appointment of a full board of directors followed, people from across Canada with knowledge of universities and sensitive to the role of academics in planning, who were dedicated to the establishment of a national university.

Another key person in this story is Denis Smith, who was not only a friend and colleague of Symons but also shared his views about this project from a unique perspective. As a lecturer in political science and a don in Devonshire College in 1957 he, with Symons and other faculty, successfully fought off attempts within the University of Toronto to sell off Devonshire House to Trinity College. As many of the arguments used in that affair had to do with the quality of education and the academic integrity of the House as a unit, they found themselves sitting around discussing the ideal university and "how great it would be to start our own university."[3] Shortly thereafter, in January 1960, Smith became the registrar of the new York University and its first paid employee, and found himself with students arriving in September. By 1962, he was one of Symons's choices for appointment to the academic planning committee for Trent because of his experience with start-up concerns. What he brought were some very strong views on the need for advance planning before start-up.

The committee was augmented by others recruited from other universities for their interest in the approach that Symons and Smith were proposing, including John Pettigrew (also from Devonshire House), Richard Sadleir, John A. MacFarlane and George Connell. A campus planning committee was formed to work in parallel with the academic planning committee, and memberships overlapped to guarantee communication. As it developed, these committees started work before they could be formally appointed because of the delay in the government's approval of the charter, so that almost three years' head start was achieved before the official appointments and charter could be confirmed in 1963.[4]

The educational philosophy of Trent was almost a given with this team at the helm. All were totally committed to a 'collegiate' system of education from their earlier discussions of 'the ideal university'. By this they meant that the members of different disciplines would live in the same College. Collegiality as a principle was to be reinforced by emphasizing teaching by seminar and tutorial rather than lecturing to a large class. The important implications of this approach for a building design are a high faculty-student ratio, and a major emphasis on teaching on the part of the faculty. They were quickly successful in winning the support of the new board to this concept. At Trent's opening ceremonies in 1964, President Symons outlined their position: *This philosophy of our university is reflected in the decision that Trent should be a collegiate university—that is, that it should be made up of a number of smaller sister colleges, which will be the fundamental units and the chief features of Trent University. Every student and faculty member at Trent will be a member of one or the other of these colleges. In this way, through the colleges, members of the university may be helped to preserve a sense of individual identity as the university grows larger, and to find richer personal associations and a greater measure of academic assistance than would otherwise be the case.*[5]

In a recent interview, Professor Symons defended the choice of the college system at Trent and the reasoning behind it: *People look to the college system and leap to the conclusion it was an import from Oxford or Harvard. These were but two of many universities whose academic programs and buildings were helpful examples.*

The driving force behind the [educational] concept of Trent was the profound concern the planning group felt about what was happening to many of the universities in Canada, particularly the enormous growth which was leading to a loss of student/faculty contact, a breakdown of collegiality amongst the faculty, and a decline in undergraduate education as more attention was given to graduate education. They were aghast at what was going on at the University of Toronto . . . the alienation of students and faculty. Academic elephantiasis was defiling Canadian universities. At Trent, collegiality, undergraduate life and education were our prime concerns.[6]

The educational approach and the importance of the close relation between teachers and students was to have a direct influence on the planning of the campus, and more particularly, the design of the buildings of the new university.

An excellent site was found situated in a wide valley on either side of the Otonabee River, three miles north of the city of Peterborough. It was located at the base of the Pre-Cambrian Shield, close to the edge of the still wild land of northern Ontario.

One of the first tasks for the new president was to complete the transactions to acquire the site and to get on with the development of a master plan for the university which would embody the "collegiate" vision that was evolving from the academic planning committee, and to work out a schedule which would allow the earliest possible start without compromising the plan. On his advice, the board decided to set aside the 1963-64 academic year for planning and developing faculty and programs, thus not accepting students until September 1964. Symons then appointed Denis Smith to the faculty and as chairman of the campus planning committee, and authorized an immediate start on the search for an architect.

The call for submissions brought responses from more than thirty architectural firms, from which five were invited to make full presentations of their work and qualifications to a selection committee of four persons and the president. Ron Thom, in Toronto and at work on Massey College, impressed the whole committee with his sensitivity, and with his approach which was in concert with what they had in mind. He won their unanimous support and the commission as partner-in-charge of the project for the Vancouver firm of Thompson, Berwick, Pratt.[7] Getting his firm to set him up in Toronto, rather than doing the job in Vancouver and commuting, was a much more difficult task for him. After considerable argument, backed up by his threats that he was going to Toronto anyway, in the spring of 1963 TBP set up an office there without delay.[8]

WITH A CLEAR ACADEMIC PHILOSOPHY and an articulate, energetic and idealistic client group mobilizing its resources for the earliest possible start—and with Massey College almost in its finishing stage—Thom was forced to make some hasty decisions about the set-up of his office, and a series of management decisions about staffing, organization and the business arrangements with the Vancouver office. The award of two high-profile university contracts in a row had established his credentials as an architect who was going to make his presence felt in Toronto, so there was no difficulty in recruiting highly talented staff. Within the first year he had hired Dick Sai-Chew, Alastair Grant, Bill Lett, Peter Smith, Don Nichol, all architects, and Bob McIntyre, a technologist, all of whom brought specialized skills and experience. The office was set up quickly, and the group soon started on the development of the Trent master plan. Molly Golby and Ron had married, and she had become essential to Thom's firm, joining the staff on a full-time basis and revealing needed managerial and administrative

skills. Ron went to Board meetings of TBP in Vancouver. Ned Pratt came every few months to Toronto to discuss work in progress, and administrative staff came when required. Things were quickly under control, and the office was up and running by the end of 1963.

The office was located at 47 Colbourne St. in downtown Toronto, near the St. Lawrence Market in a row of old four-storey brick-and-timber warehouses then still in use to store onions. The buildings offered deep loft space with high ceilings. One of these was owned by a newly formed syndicate of architects and consultants called Intake Ltd., and headed up by a lawyer, George Miller. John Andrews, an Australian architect who was becoming well-known in Toronto, had just moved into the building and started a practice. Gerald Gladstone, a prominent Toronto sculptor, occupied the basement. It was an ideal space, and Thom leased one floor. Over the next few years the proximity of other architects, including Andrews, his partners Roger duToit and Jack Diamond, and other tenants such as Evan Walker, an architect-programmer, Dick Strong, a landscape architect, and Donovan Pinker, an urban planner, provided the basis for serious interactions, moral support and critical dialogue. The complex of offices became a magnet for the best students and young architects in the area. They were also a powerful potential resource for Thom right there on his doorstep.

It was not long before Thom began to attract clients for houses in the Toronto area, which were hard to resist despite the huge workload everyone in his office was under. With such a full plate of interesting work in front of them, the whole office (ten to fifteen people) settled in with great enthusiasm and idealism to a friendly and supportive family-like ambience that was both enjoyable and productive.

According to Bob McIntyre, *there were no titles. Work was delegated directly to a person on the grounds of capability only. There were no other defined jobs . . . if the floor was dirty you swept it, everyone took the responsibility. . . the job was never complete, you kept designing on the job until the last moment . . . Ron took an interest in you, your family and how they were coming along.* [9]

That was the same year, 1963, that Canada was awarded the go-ahead for EXPO 67, leaving only four years to plan, design and build a world class exhibition, which normally takes seven years. The Russians, who had originally secured the 1967 Fair, had given up after three years, and a group of business people in Montreal, together with a design team headed by Sandy and Blanche Van Ginkel, with Michel Chevalier, convinced Mayor Jean Drapeau that a compact version of it could still be done in the remaining four years, and at the same time deal with some of Montreal's more pressing urban renewal problems. Drapeau was convinced, and quickly made the project his own, obtaining the support of the federal government. Once he had approval of the proposal, he negotiated expansion of the site and escalation of the Fair back to full-scale anyway, thus assuring the maximum residual benefits to Montreal. At this scale and with a short deadline, the project required the mobilization of all the best design talent in the country, not to mention that of the construction industry. By 1964, in the Colbourne St. building alone, Dick Strong and Donovan Pinker were hard at work on aspects of the the master plan and landscaping, and Gerry Gladstone was setting up his studio in the basement to build several enormous sculptures. John Andrews was awarded a commission for the Africa Pavilion the next year. TBP in Vancouver was awarded the contract for several service-building complexes, and

passed these over to Ron Thom.

The Colbourne St. building was a hive of EXPO activity and discussion over and above all the other work going on. It also became a drop-in centre for the more interesting designers in Toronto and from across the country on their way to and from Montreal, with the ensuing long, enthusiastic and argumentative discussions about work in progress. In addition to the EXPO projects, there was plenty to discuss. The new firm of Erickson/Massey in Vancouver had just won the competition for the overall plan and centrepiece building of Simon Fraser University in British Columbia. Andrews was just completing Scarborough College in Toronto and was moving on to the Guelph University student housing complex. Thom's work was particularly interesting in the context of these new Canadian university buildings and other new university plans from other countries appearing in the architectural press, because Massey College and Trent, with their collegiate approach, were different and unusual relative to the university planning ideas aimed at large enrolments which these other architects were exploring. To fuel the debate, everyone had an expense account, which led to many 'three martini' lunches and long dinners at the King Edward Hotel one block away.

RON AND MOLLY moved into an upper storey apartment in a house within the University of Toronto precinct, on which Ron had done a masterful job of interior conversion with B.C. cedar and Japanese gold paper ceilings, burlapped walls, painted trim in strong colours, and some tricks with windows to sneak a roof-deck up into the trees within the roof forms. It was an easy and facile demonstration of his highly developed skills for the creation of a rich living environment, and his ingenuity with renovation.

With this home base, they were in a position to entertain. Molly, with a background in literature and a continuing involvement in amateur theatre in Toronto, had a wide circle of friends, including writers, playwrights, actors, directors, producers, designers and artists. Ron's connection with Massey College, and with Trent, put him in social contact with an increasing number of academics of many disciplines and many other highly educated and interesting persons, patrons and potential clients, all interested in meeting this Westerner who had arrived on the scene and created a fine but unusual building. Thom, if not yet a celebrity, was a curiosity worth investigating, so that his and Molly's social calendar was quickly filled.

WITH HIS ARCHITECT IN PLACE, president Symons sent Thom, with Denis Smith and three members of the academic and campus planning committees, to visit eight English universities (Oxford, Cambridge, Sussex, Kent at Canterbury, East Anglia, Warwick, Lancaster and York). In a slightly unorthodox arrangement, Molly joined them. This was Thom's first exposure to England and its rich architectural resources. On their assignment, the committee members examined seventeen buildings and met with the persons responsible for them to discuss the building's performance and their experience with each of them from an operating perspective.

Trent historian A.O.C. Cole relates that at Oxford *they realized how Trent could eliminate the need for an Arts building by emphasizing the role of the colleges and designing them so that all arts teaching could take place within them. At Cambridge, they saw how pedestrian bridges across a river and buildings at the water's edge could integrate the Otonabee River and the university. From the new University of Sussex they learned that the university should not become too isolated in the country-* *side. Everywhere the full importance of site planning and control was reinforced in their thinking.*[10]

They returned with great enthusiasm for the college system as an excellent model for undergraduate education, and very knowledgeable about which building layouts reinforced it, as well as which to avoid. According to Denis Smith, *Ron Thom was impressed with the planning process of the new universities at York, Lancaster and Kent at Canterbury, but not by the architecture. For him, the old buildings at Oxford and Cambridge came through very strongly. The only new building we were all impressed by was Arne Jacobsen's St. Catherine's College at Oxford, chiefly for the refinement of detail in the building and in the interior furniture and furnishings.*[11]

On this trip Thom finally got to see the precedents for Massey College as well as those for Trent. (Whereas Massey College is unique as a strictly residential college for a select group of postgraduate students, it is not a directly applicable model for Trent, although there are similar functions.) The trip was focussed on visiting buildings which would provide useful data for the design of co-educational combined living-and-learning environments for undergraduate students entering university directly from the secondary school system. Also of interest were the new universities and their personnel, the latter for their recent experience with planning, management and construction issues.

Later in the year, Thom was sent on another tour with a different committee to visit eight American campuses (Middlebury College, Dartmouth College, Wellesley College, and the universities of MIT, Harvard, Boston, Brandeis and Yale) including twenty-one buildings, all in the New England area. From his own report on the trips[12] it is clear that Thom learned a great deal about space planning and materials, particularly from the New England colleges that had to deal with a climate similar to that of Peterborough. For him, having just arrived in Toronto from the West Coast, that knowledge was vital.

THE MEMBERS of the campus planning committee, led by Denis Smith, were starting the process of translating the academic plan for the new university into a physical plan for the site and the buildings. Initially, this involved consolidating their observations and writing a statement of their position regarding the quality of life and the environment conducive to the educational approach to which they had committed themselves. Thom spent many hours in meetings with them to come to understand their intentions, and to begin to insert some direction to the planning process. By the end of the first year all had agreed on a statement of their position with regard to the development of the campus: *We are not committed to any particular style of buildings but only to a certain spirit . . . of appropriateness and beauty which gives the kind of aesthetic stimulation and sense of repose which encourages scholarly application . . . There should be, in the design of the buildings, some intimation of the best architectural traditions of the region, as particularly expressed in the best 19th century stone farm houses, and in such buildings as the Peterborough Courthouse, Hamilton House, St. John's Church and St. Peter's Cathedral . . . We believe that this kind of deference to good regional tradition is an important part of putting down firm and live roots for the university in the community in which it is located . . . All kinds of university activity should occur throughout the campus: the colleges should be interspersed with the science buildings, and all should be easily accessible to the library, the river, playing fields, open spaces, and a small commercial village. Similarly, the design of buildings should not be so inharmonious as to suggest, for instance, a sharp distinction between a science building*

and a college. The unity of its purpose should be stated in its architecture . . . In the college system as we foresee it, there will be no single and obvious centre of university life, but many; the university library will, however, be the most important building shared by all parts of the university, and central to its purpose; its centrality should be recognized in the master plan . . . The campus should be designed for pedestrians, and buildings should be on a human scale, to complement and emphasize the university's central concern for the individual. There should be outdoor areas of congregation, such as quadrangles, walks and cloisters, and areas of isolation and unspoiled nature. The advantage of the long vistas from several parts of the campus should be made use of . . . Traffic and parking should be excluded from major areas of the campus; only service and ceremonial traffic should be permitted on the main parts of the campus; major traffic and parking should be kept on the fringes, and made unobtrusive by landscaping . . . We believe in the lasting importance of Trent University's approach to university education, and we believe in the basic role of architecture in fulfilling the university's intentions. The university should be a place of aesthetic as well as intellectual excitement.[13]

Clear indeed. As the Trent work got underway, the first buildings to be dealt with were in the downtown area of Peterborough. A decision had been taken to renovate some older large houses, and to cluster some modest new wood-frame residential buildings around them to form the first two colleges and an assembly/dining hall. This would allow an immediate start on the recruitment of faculty and the admission of the first students in the fall of 1964. The provincial government made funds available for these conversions as temporary facilities, but the committee knew that that these buildings had real quality and that the university would probably need them permanently. Those decisions on the town colleges, and Thom's renovation of them, were among the most significant early choices. They remain one of Trent's special features.

An old building nearby was acquired for a field office, and Thom brought Dick Sai-Chew, a former colleague in TBP, from Montreal and teamed him with Bob McIntyre from Toronto to set it up and supervise all the work on both sites for the duration of the Trent project. In the downtown Toronto office, Thom and his team set to work on the physical plan for the large open site on the Otonabee River, which was named the Nassau campus.

One of the first tasks was to resolve the site boundaries and designate land for specific uses. The planners had decided to provide land for future development, including that required for the university's buildings and related activities, and other sites for potential revenue-generating projects. (The foresight of the founders and planners in this regard is only now, nearly thirty years later, becoming understood and appreciated as the university is exploring specific development options for housing and commercial use to produce much-needed revenue.) Another early task was to examine the site's physical geography, micro-climate and ecology. The Otonabee River which cuts through it is part of the old Trent Canal system, which provides a route for public recreational boating. It is ideal for many water activities aside from its scenic attractiveness, and hence provides a venue for student activities central to the campus. A dam and an electrical power station on the river became the university's property as a gift from Canadian General Electric,[14] thereby providing the campus with its own power sufficient to implement an earlier planning decision to make Trent an all-electric campus, including heating. A principal feature of the site are two drumlins, large high mounds formed by

glacial action and now seen as two grass-covered low hills, located opposite each other on either side of the river. By the time these matters had been considered, the logical location for the college buildings became obvious and detailed planning could proceed.

Working diagrammatically, the architects grouped two colleges and the Library on the west shore of the river, forming the entrance to the university and a gathering place at the end of a pedestrian bridge connecting it to a smaller plaza formed by a grouping of science buildings on the east shore. The west shore group was to be surrounded by several additional colleges. A second pedestrian bridge was envisaged reaching from the same Library plaza across the river to a commercial village farther down the east shore as a focus for another group of colleges. The two nodes on the east shore would be connected by a street passing through a grouping of still further colleges, resulting in an eventual compact triangular formation for the university as a whole, with the river passing through it. Sites were identified for a possible total of twenty-one colleges. Each college would consist of a residential unit for students and some faculty families, and faculty office-seminar rooms. Most of the teaching was to take place in small group tutorials. The need for a few classrooms and lecture theatres was anticipated, and these were to be integrated into the master plan at key locations.

As the plan evolved, Thom began a series of studies to examine different approaches to building form and to the grouping of buildings to seek out their functional logic and to assess their visual impact. As well, he was evolving guidelines to govern these matters in the expectation that many different architects would eventually be involved with the design of later buildings. In a presentation to the Board summarizing his conclusions on the master plan he stated: *No attempt has been made to establish a fully definitive design of an entire university as was done with Scarborough College by Andrews in Toronto, and Simon Fraser University by Erickson in Vancouver. Instead, a major framework is being constructed that will allow change and development. Ideas will modify as buildings are built and lived and worked in. This is a healthy condition that must be facilitated. At present the plan has not explored everything in enough detail to ensure the character that the academic staff intends will necessarily grow out of it. This can only be assured when each part is studied until its exact needs are revealed. Only then can a meaningful program be written for each building. The attempt now is to find a method of building that will not be outdated, which will be consistent with modern technology and which will be sufficiently flexible to satisfy a variety of different conditions for the foreseeable future. Ultimately the planning should produce harmony without rigidity.*[15]

In a conversation at the time he was working on the site plan, Thom was discussing ways of communicating his intentions graphically. He said that: *He had drawn circles to scale on the site plan, each of an area sufficient to provide a site for a residential college for 200 persons including the faculty and teaching areas. These circles were shown overlapping to indicate that they should be packed closely, and that his intention was that their exterior walls, three to four storeys high facing each other, would form pedestrian streets that would lead to the focal space in each of the three clusters.*[16]

The combined effect would have been that of three villages, with their cores attached to each other by two bridges and a road. This particular diagram never made it into the guidelines. However, a small diagram of the complete site plan did appear in the magazine *Architectural Record*,[17] which indicates the principle discussed here, showing elongated free-

93

78

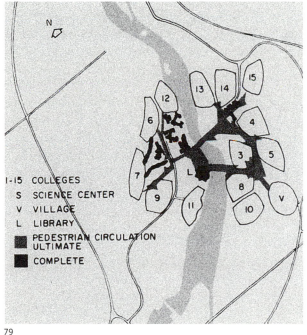

79

Figure 78
Conceptual site plan developed by Thom with the Planning committee. Each circle is drawn to scale and illustrates a site of sufficient area for one college. The sites are grouped in three clusters which would house at their core major facilities such as the library, auditoria, bus terminals, coffee shops, and so on, all three connected by bridges or major footpaths within a ten-minute walking distance.

Figure 79
The site plan as shown in *Architectural Record* was obviously developed after the first two colleges were planned and one of the major linking bridges was designed, as it shapes the site allocations to suggest a network of major and minor pathways or streets between and connections to the new buildings.

form shapes much like the plan of Lady Eaton College, with the long sides of adjacent colleges roughly parallel, suggesting either major or minor streets between.

Another part of Thom's work at this time involved the selection of a palette of materials for the exterior of the buildings which would allow some freedom for the architects but at the same time maintain a harmonious relationship between elements of the resulting whole. In collaboration with the consulting structural engineer for the whole project, Morden Yolles, Thom settled on concrete as a the most practical and versatile building material, and then experimented with different admixes of broken stone aggregates and other means to produce textural variation on the surface. All of these were used in the first buildings which he designed. Some of these applications proved to be labour intensive and therefore too costly to allow their practical use in later buildings.[18]

Once the master plan for the new campus was approved, together with all the design guidelines and the material palette, design development of the first five buildings could proceed quickly. Teams were set up for each project, headed by one of the senior associates—Bill Lett, Alastair Grant and Peter Smith—with Thom as both lead designer and critic. Thom also brought Paul Merrick from Vancouver to supplement the team. He and Thom were very close friends, and Paul had stepped into Ron's shoes at TBP in Vancouver, working closely with Ned Pratt. Merrick was versatile and hence immediately useful, leaving a strong imprint on everything he was involved with, particularly the Library, the bridge, and the Science complex.

THESE FIRST BUILDINGS were unusual and remarkable, as was the concept of the university—all equally brave statements about an ideal, humanistic education. The continuing close involvement of President Symons throughout the first phase of the building program and his focus on a creative solution can be seen in this response to a question about his interaction with the architect: *Ron had the habit of coming to me at the beginning of each building project and asking "for my instructions". . . I told him I had no instructions but I had a request . . . I hoped that he would be kind enough to join a committee of faculty, students, and others that were thinking through the functions, purpose and direction of the building, and that he would sit and listen to these discussions, and that he would not put a line on paper for a year!! . . . In the specific case of the bridge . . . I told him I wanted a bridge that students could write songs about, sing songs about, and make love on for a thousand years . . . in addition to whatever else it is supposed to do!!*

Some time after the buildings were completed and published, Symons received a telephone call from a man he had never met nor heard of, who said that he had seen a picture of the bridge and was so intrigued he came from afar to see it. *He was phoning to say that he 'took such pleasure in the bridge he wanted to help pay for it,' saying that 'a university that had the courage to insist on and encourage the aesthetic factor deserved support,' and that 'he was sending us a very substantial gift!!'*[19] Here was tangible and unique support plus further confirmation for Thom that his ideas and approach to the making of architecture were both acceptable and appreciated.

Figure 80
The bridge across the
Otonabee, looking toward
Champlain College

Figure 81
Champlain College

Figure 82
1994 site plan:
1 Bata Library
2 Bus Stop
3 Lady Eaton College
4 Champlain College
5 Bridge
6 Otonabee River
7 Earth Sciences Building
8 Chemistry Buildings
9 Auditorium
10 Otonabee College

Champlain College

Figure 83
One of the residential wings is
built at the water's edge.

Figure 84
A close-up of the exposed
aggregate surface of the walls.

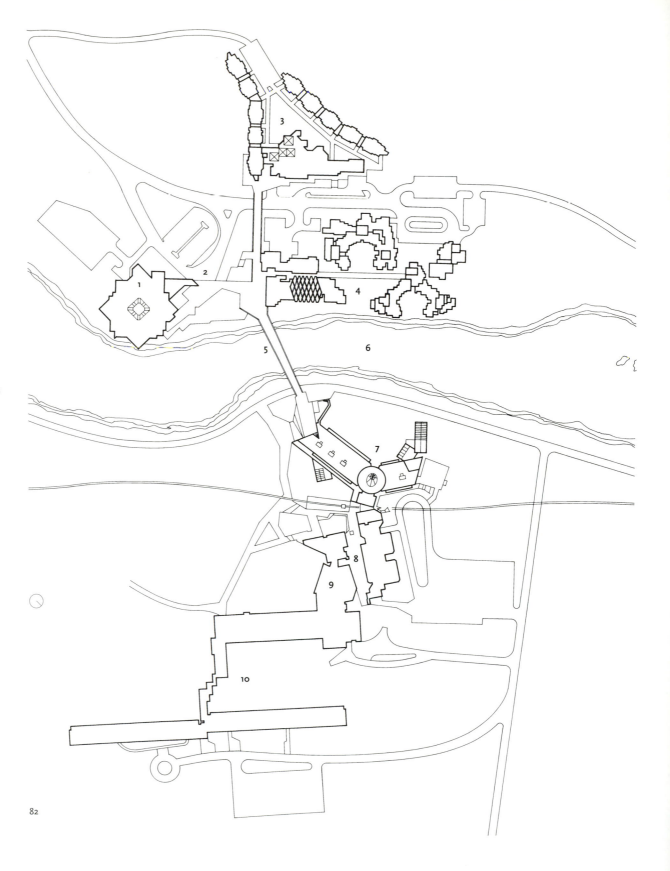

83

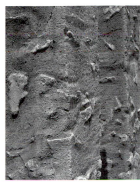

99

84

85

Champlain College

Figure 85
A vine-covered wooden Trellis over the central walkway connects the tower, the residential buildings and the classrooms to the Dining Hall and stairs up to the bridge. The tower-like configuration of the residential buildings is seen clearly here, resulting from the vertical organization of the clusters of rooms served by glass-enclosed stairtowers.

Figure 86
The buttresses at the base of the dining hall windows.

Figure 87
The Dining Hall from the water side. This building is also used on other occasions for a range of purposes, as a formal or informal assembly place for special events such as a convocation, dance or workshop.

87

86

Bata Library

Figure 88
The top-lit central atrium and stair connect all floors and organize the circulation at all levels.

Figure 89
The Bata Library and the stairs connecting the bus stop to the University Court. The University Court is the gathering place and the central hub of the campus. This outdoor plaza is on the roof of the central power-plant at the level of the bridge, approximately fifteen feet above grade. The connection to Champlain College is made here as well.

89

90

Bata Library

Figure 90
The bridge (lower right) comes ashore at the University Court, but the deck continues over the central power plant to finish at Lady Eaton College.

Lady Eaton College

Figure 91
The sculptural form of Lady Eaton College is seen here, end on. The change in the surface of the concrete walls, poured in place but without the stone aggregates that give Champlain College its unique quality, gives this building its own character. The college sits at the base of one of the drumlins, a glacial formation left from the ice age in the form of a large mound, big enough to be an interesting backdrop as seen here, but not so big as to be inaccessible. This is one of two on the campus, and it is currently being reforested to bring it back to its earlier condition.

Figure 92
The oval courtyard is private and quiet, away from the activity at the hub.

91

92

Immediate interest and acclaim for Trent came from the architectural press in several major profusely illustrated articles in important journals in Canada, Britain and the United States.[20] In one of these, Arthur Erickson, at the end of a laudatory commentary on the project in a review just after it was completed, must have had a premonition, probably based on his own earlier experience with Simon Fraser University in Vancouver, when he wrote: *Trent, at this stage, has everything going for it to become a landmark—an inspired plan, an evocative setting, a unique collection of buildings which, if it is possible, show greater mastery with each addition, and already it has gained that most elusive of all qualities, an ambience, to which everyone responds. These are great qualities but one cannot be deluded into thinking that they are not fragile ones. Thom must finish the remainder of the central part of the university, and especially all the edges on the river, in order to firmly establish his vision of the university. A misstep now, at the core, could easily undo much of what has been accomplished through great care and sensitivity. One hopes that other architects that may be commissioned to design other colleges on the periphery of the campus will have sufficient sensitivity to the quality already established. But Thom himself is the only one who can see and make real his special vision which has given Trent what they had originally expected in their architecture, as well as indefinable qualities of immeasurable value.*[21] For some reason this did not happen.

Starting at about this time and continuing over the next decade, the idealistic vision of the founders of Trent and the first buildings of the new university were subjected to the test of use, and increasingly intensive scrutiny as a result of the coincidence of a number of external and internal developments. This is not to say that Trent was singled out. Most of the problems under scrutiny in the 1970s were in some way common to all Canadian universities.[22]

Change was in the air. The whole founding team of academics and others had moved on to other positions, either in Trent or elsewhere, and were no longer in direct control of events, nor in a position to continually defend their decisions. Enrolment steadily increased, bringing in new faculty and students each year, most of whom had no previous contact with the collegiate teaching environment or approach. Many of the teachers had to relearn how to teach and counsel students, and to adjust their approach and priorities between teaching and research.

The pace of enrolment was exceeding projections, and there were not enough bed-study rooms in the five colleges on two campuses to sustain the residential aspect of the collegiate idea, nor were the seminar rooms in these colleges adequate to maintain the essential tutorial teaching mode to the extent envisaged, and larger classes by lecture increased. The enrolment was creeping over three to its target of four thousand students, for which the master plan called for fourteen or more Colleges. Only five were in place. More and more students had to find housing in Peterborough and so become day-student commuters. While commuters had been anticipated in the planning, the projected ratio between commuters and residents of 1:3 was reversed, and all the facilities and services became overcrowded.

The provincial government's funding could not keep pace with the demand across the province for both operating and capital needs. Their demographers saw a slump in enrolment coming at the end of the 1970s as this generation passed through the system, and they were busily planning for a shift in resources to other sectors of the sytem.

At Trent, a Department of Physical Plant was created as a matter of necessity, to deal with the day-to-day operation of the buildings, and the need to solve

Figure 93
The bridge and the east side of the river. The bridge, at its east end, lands at the doorstep of the new (1992) Earth Sciences building (designed by Richard Henriquez), which in turn, provides internal and external connections to the earlier Physics and Chemistry buildings (done by Ron Thom), and further up the slope to Otonabee College (done by Macy DuBois).

maintenance problems immediately. Inevitably, and correctly, it gradually took over more and more control of building decisions within the new administration. One of its early decisions was to build a one-storey staging building, essentially a low-cost but tidy one-storey office building. Neither the materials nor the site location follow the guidelines or the master plan, and the protestations of Thom as campus planner were overruled. This decision, however expedient, undercut his effectiveness in any subsequent monitoring or control of future developments. The building was needed to accommodate administrative departments and to house new academic units as they came on campus and waited for their final assigned location. Unfortunately, it also delayed their initiation into the collegiate system. The general shortage of space required faculty to rely on the lecture system with large classes, thus not participating in seminar instruction to the same extent. Internal discussions started within the Trent faculty as to academic direction, shifting some of the teaching program away from the tutorial system, particularly in the new sciences.

Otonabee College was built at about the same time as the original buildings were nearing completion. The university, under the pressures described above, decided to build this new college for 400 students, stretching the budget wherever possible. It was located on the slope above the developing Science complex on the east side of the river. Twice the size of the other colleges, it is out of scale with the original buildings, but by its siting on higher ground it does not entirely prevent the realization of the intent of the original plan, in that at least one new college could still be built between it and the river. Otonabee College was the first project to go to another architect, Macy Dubois, and it provided the second test of the design guidelines. The building is out of character with Thom's buildings (it is linear in its organization), and the materials used do not follow the guidelines as they were set out, which indicates that the seeds of change had already put down substantial roots.

In a paper given at the International College and University Conference in Atlantic City in 1970, Thom reflected on Trent's developing problems: *When Massey College was designed in 1961 none of these concerns [about burgeoning enrolment and scarce financial resources] was very apparent. Massey College was fully funded by a private Foundation, and designed to be built by traditional methods of construction, including some which were hand-crafted. Its entire concern was to provide for a community of scholars, all post-graduates, whose work involved them in other parts of the University of Toronto, who would live and study in the College . . . Little was overlooked to create a complete environment appropriate to the life expected to go on within . . . The result has been most satisfactory to the College. It has functioned well, but as its cost per bed was almost $20,000, it cannot be considered an answer to the present problem of building universities.*

Trent University, coming two years later, held very similar academic ideals. Founded in 1963, it was built during the period of rapid, almost witless expansion of Ontario universities. Like Massey College, it was designed to accommodate roughly similar academic patterns. Unlike Massey College, it was financed largely by the Province; consequently its cost per bed was (about) half in spite of some inflation in the meantime.

From the earliest planning stages of Trent, we sought to establish a building vernacular that belonged with the region, and that was sufficiently economical not to have to be abandoned in the future . . . The use of crushed stone poured in walls with concrete was anticipated to serve indefinitely as a viable building method . . . But it didn't. Neither did a number of planning decisions that were made at the outset . . . The attempts to transpose some traditional academic and social patterns into a middle class North American context were not always successful, and modifications to the original thoughts will be required in several areas as the campus develops. As with Massey, much of Trent is valid still and should remain so indefinitely, since the basic human being is slow to change, even when his environment is changing rapidly.

A combination of continued inflation and an antiquated building system, however, has made short work of the chosen building technology . . . Only seven years after its founding, Trent is having to re-assess its financial and physical structures, and in some cases its social and educational structures. This is no fault of Trent, which has spent great effort planning. It is an inevitable product of the rate of change.[23]

By 1972 Thom had completed the projects for which he had been commissioned and was not involved in further developments at Trent. The campus as originally visualized remains incomplete. While Thom put a brave front on his disappointment it is not illogical to conclude that his increasing despondency about the conditions of practice as an architect in the next few years originated with this experience.

THERE IS NO DOUBT that Trent University, notwithstanding periods of adversity and perpetual underfunding, has established its presence and unique character among Canadian universities. It is academically strong and healthy, and the graduates have come away with a distinctive stamp, despite the necessary shift from idealism to a more pragmatic approach in some aspects of the enterprise. A detailed tour of the campus today reflects the destructive effects of overcrowding and inadequate maintenance over a quarter-century, but discussions with current faculty and staff reflect the awakening

of awareness of the true extent and seriousness of the problem. A new round of funding has resulted in the completion of a new Environmental Sciences building beautifully sited to link Thom's Chemistry and Physics buildings on the east bank to the pedestrian bridge, and from there, across the river to the Library complex on the west side. Designed by Richard Henriquez of Vancouver, it sets an idiosyncratic but instantly popular precedent for the next round of building. While demonstrating sensitivity to Thom's master plan, the architect has shown great skill in handling the difficult problems of scale, connection, form and siting. The resulting complex reinforces the core of the plan, establishing the sense of connectedness and interdependence of the east and west components of the university by resolving the continuity of the circulation system, linking old and new levels and pathways thus maintaining previous access as well as providing additional routes.

A more modest further building program for the university than that envisaged by the founders is both probable and achievable, together with a program of repair, restoration and minor additions to existing plant. An impressive expanded program of reforestation is underway as originally planned. All of this will have to respond to an evolving academic program and economic climate, as well as a changing student mix within the university. The lessons deriving from the very thorough planning process initiated by the founders who included Ron Thom in their deliberations from the beginning, particularly the importance of the connection between the academic ideals and the resulting architecture, are well understood and being taken very seriously, which bodes well for the immediate future.

10 Transition

EXPO 67 TOOK PLACE in Montreal in 1967 as the central feature of our national Centennial celebrations. It was a once-in-a-lifetime chance to show the world what Canadians could do. Expo 67 was a celebration of many things, probably the most important of which was a belief system that had evolved during the postwar period in the western world and which underlay the spirit of the fair, without being made explicit. Building on the tenet enshrined in Jefferson's Declaration of Independence that "all men are created equal," came new beliefs arising out of the scientific, technological and social revolution of the early postwar period that man is perfectable, and that man will ultimately control the universe. These beliefs also underlay popular faith in the notion of 'progress'. The wide public impact of the knowledge explosion and the revolution in information technology propagated these beliefs. There were reports of something new every day: new inventions, processes, nuclear power, wonder materials, new transportation systems (turbo, then jet, then rocket propulsion), transistors to microchips, electronics to computers. Everything was possible.

Expo 67 was one audio-visual extravaganza. Exhibits displayed every new technological invention, and their designers revelled in the opportunity to communicate the beginnings of a global perspective in new ways. The outstanding exhibition buildings were: the United States Pavilion, a huge geodesic dome designed by Buckminster Fuller (the prophet of it all) complete with prototypes of the actual Apollo 'moon-shot' travel vehicles; Moshe Safdie's Habitat demonstration housing project; and the theme buildings designed by Guy Desbarats of ARCOP Architects—Man the Explorer and Man the Producer. These four projects were selected for major coverage in the prestigious international architectural publications as prototypes of the 'megastructure,'[1] a concept for very large mixed-use general-purpose buildings, which was then under hot discussion as the solution to urban renewal. Three of these four buildings were designed by Canadians, and this fact did not go unnoticed. That international recognition inaugurated a new phase in the development of large scale Canadian architecture in the 1970s and, at least initially, boosted the confidence of Ron Thom's generation of architects.

A reaction to twenty-five years of uninhibited postwar progress was inevitable, as people of all stripes tried to absorb the meaning and implications for them of such rapid change while experiencing its side-effects. By the end of the 1960s, the storm warnings of a recession and evidence of a profound social revolution were clearly visible on the streets and in the media of the major countries of the western world. The burning of the ghettoes in Detroit and Watts, the Cuban missile crisis, the Vietnam War, the student revolt in the United States and Europe, the civil liberties battles, the re-awakening of the feminist movement and the emergence of the counter-cultures, were only some of the indicators that a strong reaction was brewing.

THE THOMPSON, BERWICK, PRATT FIRM in Vancouver had been reorganized in 1964 in response to its expanding workload just as Thom had opened the Toronto office to complete Massey College and start on Trent. TBP took on two new senior partners, both engineers, to share responsibility and expand in-house specialist service capability. During the following year, Dave Hickman was delegated to enter into discussions with all the partners about the detailed organization of the new partnership, and to develop options. A subject of great interest was the notion of cost centres, with each partner having responsibility for a specific centre. Thom, with Trent as a client and more than $20 million worth of projects in front of him, was one of these. He followed the organizational discussions closely with his own staff, and was on the phone regularly with ideas and questions.

For some time, he had been trying to persuade the Vancouver office to release Bob Murtrie to assist him with administration and management matters. They did so in 1967, and for the next three years Thom and Murtrie worked to sort out the problems of the Toronto office, and to define their version of an appropriate model for the new corporate firm which would place the Toronto office in a growth position. In addition to internal discussions, on their own initiative they brought in management consultants to review and help clarify several options. One very ambitious option Thom was keen on was to build a trans-Canada firm based on the highly successful Skidmore, Owings and Merrill practice in the United States. They went so far as to discuss an alliance with Ray Affleck in Montreal, which he dismissed rather offhandly, saying that "second generation firms do not work!"[2] Thom and Murtrie continued their studies and commenced to prepare a submission to the TBP partnership outlining five options, ranging from an integrated partnership to complete separation.

While he liked the idea of being responsible for a specific unit, Thom had no training in the management of a large budget and was not prepared for the corporate style of the new partnership with its inevitable monitoring of his operation to guarantee its efficiency in the pursuit of profit. After four years of bickering between Vancouver and Toronto over these matters, one of the new senior partners, Otto Safir, reviewed Thom's accounts and the Toronto operation and was "upset and annoyed that Ron could have lost so much money considering the projects

he had to work with."[3] Thom had many times at previous meetings been openly contemptuous of and raged at "technocrats and bureaucrats" who interfered in his operation. In the words of one witness, "the tension in the board meetings was unbelievable . . . Thom's personal dislike of one or two of the partners was palpable. He was not mentally structured to deal with a corporate partnership . . . he was too much an individualist. [He and the firm] had to separate, however regrettable."[4]

As Ned Pratt puts it, "hubris was surfacing on Ron's part."[5] At meetings of the new board, Thom found himself having to answer for the financial performance of his operation to an efficiency-minded, corporate-oriented new mix of people. He now had fewer friends at the table. The dissension came to a head in 1970 with the completion of Trent. Thom asked the board to consider the five options he and Murtrie had developed for the restructuring of the firm. After a short discussion, the board decided to proceed with the complete separation of the Toronto office and to phase out Thom's partnership, setting out a schedule for the transition. Thom was henceforth on his own. Murtrie left the firm.

IN 1968, PRIOR TO THE SEPARATION of the two firms, and just as the Vancouver firm was reorganizing, the provincial government announced a major project with a proposal call to facilitate the selection of architects. The project involved the creation of a government centre in the heart of downtown Vancouver, by the construction of a fifty-five-storey office complex for government and private sector offices, and by the renovation and expansion of the Provincial Courthouse, all on a two-block site. Ned Pratt set out to win this competition and included Ron Thom's involvement as partner and designer to bolster his proposal, even though Thom was located in Toronto. Pratt did win, but on the condition (at the client's insistence) that Thom be the lead designer, and that Pratt accept a joint-venture partnership with another Vancouver firm, McCarter and Nairne. In the initial stages, Thom was only nominally involved. However, as the project moved into the design stage, his status with TBP had changed, and he was then on his own in Toronto. The government's Chief Architect, George Giles, would not accept this change without adjustment, and so the joint-venture was revised to include the three firms, with the two Vancouver firms each involved in design, and Thom cast in the role of design co-ordinator with the final say on design decisions, commuting as required. Pratt installed Paul Merrick as his firm's designer.

The project went through two distinct phases as it passed through preliminary design, and hardened up in the following detailed development stage. Thom became interested in the tower, which was being developed by the McCarter and Nairne team, and made a major input into its design, working with Ron Nairne and Blair MacDonald. The tower was not only tall (55 stories), it also had a very large floor plate (20,000 square feet), and the building was therefore bulky despite the refined treatment of its exterior surfaces. What was clear at this stage was that the underlying problem with the project was the overloading of the two-block site by the required amount of accommodation. This situation had been identified by the design team during the preliminary design phase. Proposals were made as to how to solve this problem, but they were ignored by the provincial government client, in a hurry to get the project in the ground before an election was called, and after a belated attempt to get financial participation and additional site area from the City of Vancouver had failed.

As the whole project was approaching approval to proceed with the detailed production phase, Merrick (who was in charge of the Courthouse complex), with the approval of Pratt, unilaterally decided to look at alternatives that would reduce the apparent bulk of the tower, even though any such modification required the agreement of Thom and the McCarter and Nairne team before a proposal could be placed before the Minister. As it developed, Merrick ran out of time, and while he was only able to discuss it briefly with Thom who was not enthusiastic, he decided to bring forward a proposal for a redesigned tower based on a triangular floor plan at a meeting involving the Minister and in the presence of the whole architectural group. When he did, Giles, as chairman, immediately asked Pratt if this was an alternate design proposal. Pratt was caught off-guard, but he responded that "they should rather consider it to be a minority report."[6] Giles then asked Thom, as design co-ordinator, for his opinion. Thom, too, was caught, and whatever he thought, he had no alternative but to support the McCarter and Nairne design and the continuation of the originally agreed project because the proposal had not been discussed and endorsed by the three firms. Giles, an experienced chairman, called a recess during which he persuaded Pratt, who was angry with Thom, to make unanimous the agreement to continue. When the meeting resumed and Merrick heard the decision, to Pratt's consternation, he said, "because I did not get the support of my colleagues for this proposal, I will have to resign from the design team."[7] Some time later, Giles persuaded him, too, to continue his involvement.

The project did continue into full working drawings on a fast track schedule, and was on the verge of going to contract when the government lost the election. The incoming government stopped work on

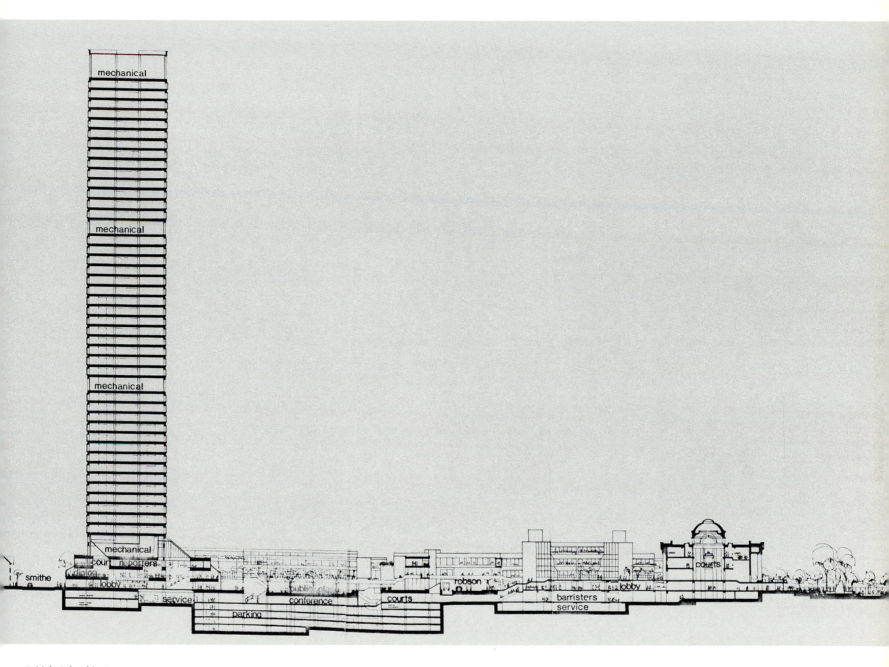

Labels within the figure:
mechanical

mechanical

mechanical

mechanical
court reporters
smithe
dialog
lobby
service
parking
public place
conference
courts
robson
barristers
service
lobby
courts

**British Columbia Government
Centre, Vancouver**

Figure 94
Longitudinal section through
two city blocks, the tower and
the court house.

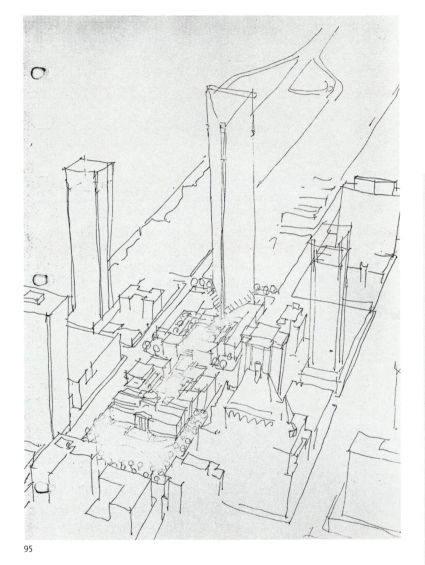

95

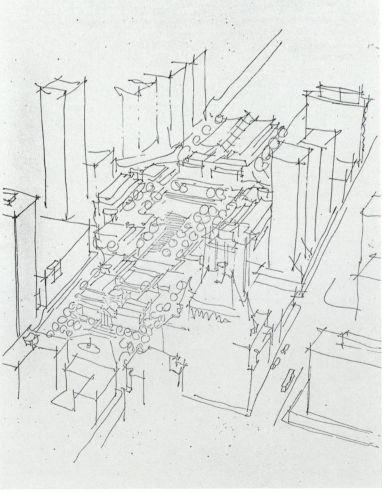

96

Figure 95
The sketch illustrates Merrick's triangular tower alternative to the 55 storey tower under development at that time, with supposedly the same floor area.

Figure 96
The sketch is of a hypothetical low-rise complex for the whole Government Centre spread over three blocks instead of the two allocated. The sketch is the result of Merrick's private musing about the project, but curiously, it appears to anticipate Arthur Erickson's final solution built later for a newly elected and very different provincial NDP government, led by Dave Barrett, which defeated the Socred government of W.A.C. Bennett.

it, and, after changing the program and enlarging the site allocation, commissioned Arthur Erickson as sole architect for the project.

The principals of all three of the original firms shook their heads in disbelief at the irony of the outcome. Nairne, however, was philosophical. When the topic comes up, Pratt still rages against Thom for failing to support Merrick and his old firm, which is surprising considering that the firm had severed its relationship to Thom in the midst of the job. His attitude also ignores the extent of Thom's involvement, made in good faith, in the design of the tower Pratt and Merrick were trying to scrap. Thom was surprised that Pratt was surprised, given the circumstances, but was more depressed to have lost the project to his, by then, arch-rival, Erickson. Merrick was relieved that the tower was never built, but he, too, carried a grudge against his good friend Thom for some time.

Here, then, is a classic case of a flawed program for a huge project, given excellent management at the operational level, but a forced marriage in the design group—a recipe for disaster. Thom, who was uncertain about his position when he was forced into the project by his partnership with Pratt, was then given the key design leadership role when he became a free agent in 1970. Even then, because of his location in Toronto and the demands of a new office there, he was still not close enough to the day-to-day pulse of the design process to prevent the split within the design group on the fundamental approach to the design of the tower. This was a no-win situation for him.

FOR THOM, the disappointing, anticlimactic ending of the Vancouver project was offset by the parallel need to get on with the organization of his own firm to deal with a sudden influx of new work in Ontario,

which was coming his way as a direct result of the completion of Massey College and Trent University. The publicity from these projects had given him a high profile in Toronto with the client world there. From the time of severance from the Vancouver firm in 1970, over the next three years he completed six important and prominent buildings for each of which he was the principal designer. These projects consolidated his reputation and established his independence.

The timing of Thom's severance from the Vancouver firm, coming just as he was getting involved with the B.C. Government complex, had raised immediate problems in the Toronto office. His full attention was needed to focus on ongoing problems of payroll, transition, carryover projects and new contracts, and on major decisions on what kind of an office organization he wanted for an independent firm. The staff numbers had been steadily increasing since 1966, and when they went beyond twenty people there had been a noticeable change away from the informal atmosphere that had prevailed—and there was a need to review that as well.

One model open to him was to become the sole owner and principal, perhaps with 'associates'. He had stated that his ambition was to do a lot of work. That arrangement would have made him a functional figurehead, requiring that he be involved in every project, and that he carry the sole burden of job promotion and liability as well as retain control of the thing he liked to do and did best, design. Instead he developed a least-change scenario, a model based on the way he had always worked, opting for a partnership. Continuing the firm name as "Ronald J. Thom, Architects," he offered a financial interest with full project control and some liability to his associates while maintaining an overall quality control function for himself. This arrangement would enable him to concentrate on design, and override his partners decision if necessary from his point of view. His key associates from the old firm— Alastair Grant, Peter Smith and Dick Sai-Chew— all accepted his invitation to become partners. At the time, he was still attracting more than enough work, so the new partners appear to have assumed that there was no imperative to assign specific responsibilities or to develop a strategy for the firm's own long-term development. If so, this turned out to be a serious mistake.

A MAJOR ECONOMIC DOWNTURN, the first since the end of the war, occurred in 1971, the first indicator of many to come about the new fiscal environment which would change the way the building industry would be operating in Canada, and how the architect's role and share in that industry would be changing. This went largely unnoticed in Thom's office because it was fully engaged in the completion of carryover projects, and in major projects for a new class of post-secondary educational institutions, including planning and buildings for Lester B. Pearson College of the Pacific in Victoria, B.C., two campuses of Sir Sanford Fleming College in Peterborough, Ontario, and other high profile projects in Ontario such as the Prince Hotel in Toronto, the Queen's University Social Sciences Centre in Kingston, the Shaw Festival Theatre in Niagara-on-the-Lake, and the Metro Toronto Zoo. For all of these projects Thom was fully involved as principal designer, even though several of them were done in joint-ventures with other firms.

The work on Trent University and the B.C. Government building, despite its ups and downs, had prepared Thom and his partners thoroughly for these new projects, and they were all ready and enthusiastic about getting them underway. Each of the partners except Thom became a project manager for one or more of them, backed up with a staff team which included one or more design architects, persons capable of taking a concept or rough sketch and notes from Ron Thom and developing them into a viable building in close collaboration with him. As with an orchestra, the leadership role calls for mastery and creative vision, and the ability to draw the maximum performance from others. On these projects, Thom took his role very seriously and worked very closely with each of the client groups and design teams through every stage of the project's development. In notes he put together for a lecture, he wrote: *We [the members of the team] excel in different areas . . . even within what is broadly called design—some are more technically oriented—others more visually oriented—some more towards dealing with work on site—and some to the very real ingredients such as economics and even politics. The best results occur when there is an exchange from the beginning to the end of the process between all involved representing this cross-section of abilities. This is admitting that a direction must be established—an attitude taken about a particular solution. It also says that any approach to a particular situation must be responsible to all of these areas which, whether we like it or not, ultimately effect the end product.*[7]

With the exception of the Prince Hotel, these projects were all low-to-medium-cost buildings. The characteristic of all of them is their direct, functionally-determined planning, excellent siting, their no-frills expression relying on sensible, low-maintenance materials, good proportions and restraint. There are no extravagant feature spaces. They represent the best of Thom's firm's modernist institutional work during the early 1970s. It was not until mid-decade that the firm had to face the new competitive climate for architectural work.

Lester B. Pearson College of the Pacific
The Thom Partnership in joint venture with Downs, Archambault, Architects

Figure 97
The entrance to the dining room.

Lester B. Pearson College of the Pacific

Figure 98
The interior of the dining room.

Figure 99
The interior of the student counselling room in the Administration building.

Figure 100
The Administration building clearly illustrates the steep slope of the forest terrain.

98

99

102

101

Prince Hotel
The Thom Partnership and
Reno Negrin and Associates,
Architects

Figure 101
Balcony details.

Figure 102
Tower and entrance.

Figure 103
Tower from poolside.

104

105

Arts and Social Science Complex, Queen's University
The Thom Partnership, Architects

Figure 104
Rendering. The sketch, an aerial view of the complex, illustrates the ingenious use of linked, low buildings as a means of adding to and connecting the existing higher buildings strung along an existing road. The road was closed and changed to a court-yard for pedestrians. The resulting solution Thom proposed and built thus maintains the human scale of the univer-

sity campus instead of con-fronting the students with one huge building towering over the others.

Figure 105
Entrance to Music Hall.

Figure 106
Entrance to Academic Complex.

107

108

Arts and Social Science Complex, Queen's University

Figure 107
The connecting interior street at second floor level.

Figure 108
The main courtyard, replacing the closed street.

Shaw Festival Theatre
The Thom Partnership, Architects

Figure 109
Interior. This theatre has been lauded for its intimacy and excellent acoustics. These characteristics come about from the steep pitch of the floors and the curvature of the rows of the seating, both of which reduce the distance between the actor and the audience. The ceiling and walls are BC cedar which contributes to the quality of the acoustics and adds richness to the colour and texture of the whole space.

111

Metro Toronto Zoo
The Thom Partnership in joint
venture with Clifford and
Laurie, Architects, and Craig
and Boake, Architects

Figures 110 and 111
Thom's principal involvement
in this complex project was as
a design consultant, in which
capacity he was involved with
the principal zoologists and
other consultants in all the site
planning, considering climate
and other ecological problems
in defining an appropriate
habitat for each species, the
sequence, circuits, transportation and safety of the staff and
the public, the nature and
design of the major focal places
and buildings for the presentation of the animals. The huge
polygonal structures with their
metal and translucent curved
roof surfaces serve, in addition
to their primary function, as
memorable images of location
and focus in this sprawling site.

128

Figure 112
Ron Thom, lecturing at the
Firehall Theatre, which he
designed, ingeniously trans-
forming an old firehall to
house an energetic and
resourceful amateur theatre
company.

Thom's new freedom of choice made his com-
ings and goings and the condition he would be in
when he got back somewhat unpredictable. He was
drinking heavily, and this behaviour was beginning
to make his partners feel nervous, particularly if it
overlapped with a meeting with a client.

Thom's statement that it was his ambition "to
do a lot of work," was a goal consistent with his lin-
gering conviction that the work would just flow in
the door. His then new partners tried to convince
him that the firm should take less work, and do it
better, and that the number of staff should be kept
down so that the office atmosphere could be more
informal. By the mid-1970s external factors soon
brought a different view to both of these ambitions.

11   Houses East

FLUSH WITH RECENT SUCCESSES and with a majority interest and partners in an independent, reorganized firm, Thom could pick and choose where he put his efforts. He could involve himself in key decisions in those projects that attracted him, and which offered him the most scope for his ideas. At the same time, he was assured that the projects would be looked after conscientiously by his partners. Over and above the still-major demands of the practice, he was in demand as a semi-celebrity at conferences and seminars, and as a critic at schools of architecture, all of which kept him away from the office. He was invited to sit on juries and write articles and critiques for the architectural press. Additionally, he could not resist people who wanted him to design a house for them, despite the fact he had not gotten around to setting up a team in the office to produce houses as he had done so successfully in Vancouver. In Toronto, houses were an expensive distraction which an already busy office could not really afford.

While the change in clientship of the commercial and institutional world was creating major concerns for the partners regarding the future of the firm, there was no shortage of would-be clients wanting to have Ron Thom design a house for them. He was adamant in defence of this situation: *Ever since my office was established in Toronto it has maintained an involvement with houses, and we intend to continue to do so as long as the work is there. The effect of this work on the spirit and direction of an architectural office is magic. Because the ingredients of any architectural project are all there, and because it is a more direct subject to deal with—one client—smaller size—the process from start to completion is quicker. [Everyone] sees the seed planted and the flower blossom.*[1]

For the period from 1964-75, the firm's records held in the University of Calgary Archives list forty-eight house projects done by the Toronto firm, mostly in Ontario. Many of these are substantial houses, but many are renovations and additions as separate projects. Some of these latter projects are very small, of a size that Thom could easily design and draw up in an evening at home, or, not infrequently, over a bottle of wine while talking to the clients. Some others were very large, and more than one completely developed set of working drawings for quite different schemes suggests that the original versions were sometimes too elaborate and costly, and that more modest versions were ultimately built or that the contract was terminated.

An additional thirteen projects are listed for the six following years, indicating that Thom still took them on despite his deteriorating health. He started all of them, but not all of them came to fruition.[2] Some were completed by others in the office. Some of them were built from Thom's notes and sketches made on the job, long since lost. His compulsion to do this work, whether or not it was listed by the office as a formal project, suggests he did it for its therapeutic value in restoring his self-confidence. The work was familiar and manageable, and the one-to-one relationship with the client allowed him to again experience the deep satisfaction that comes from the client's adulation while watching the 'master' at work. The Fraser house and the Frum house illustrate the two extremes. The first was done under Thom's guidance but handled fully by selected staff. The second house was done almost entirely by him, with few formal drawings and most decisions made together with the client on the site.

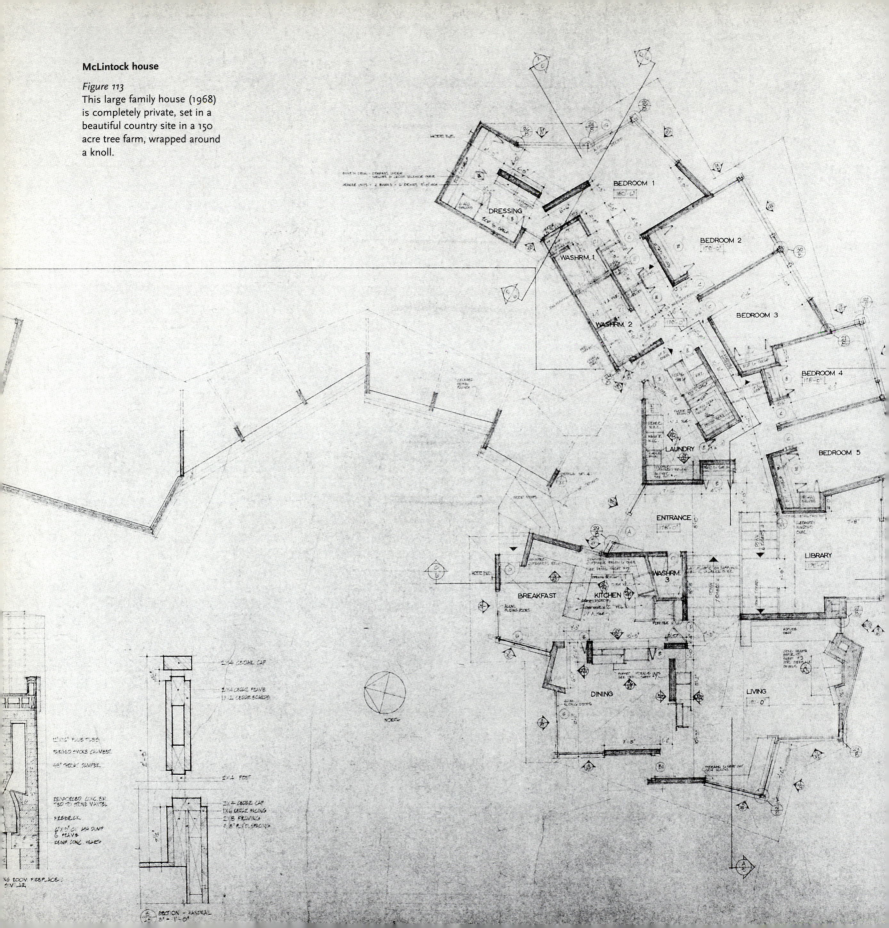

McLintock house

Figure 113
This large family house (1968) is completely private, set in a beautiful country site in a 150 acre tree farm, wrapped around a knoll.

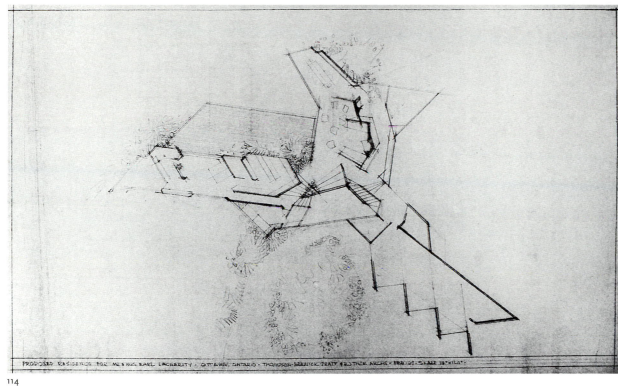

PROPOSED RESIDENCE FOR MR & MRS EARL LACHARITY · OTTAWA, ONTARIO · THOMPSON-BERWICK-PRATT & RJ THOM ARCHS · FEB '67 · SCALE 1/8"=1'0"

114

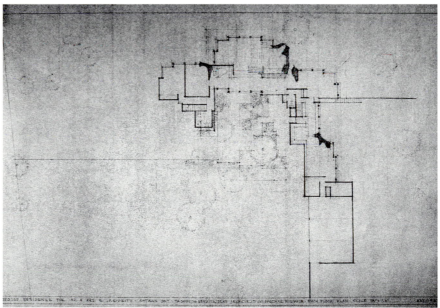

115

Sketch plan drawings by
Ron Thom

Lacharity house 1

Figure 114
The first scheme (1967)
appears to be a conversation
piece to extract from the client
a reaction to an irregular free-
form plan (not built).

Lacharity house 2

Figure 115
The second scheme (three
months later) is much more
conservative in the manner of
Frank Lloyd Wright's Oak Park
houses. However, Thom has
overdrawn unusual free-form
fireplaces which appear as
afterthoughts, but which indicate his continuing search for
form as the project matures
(no record of construction).

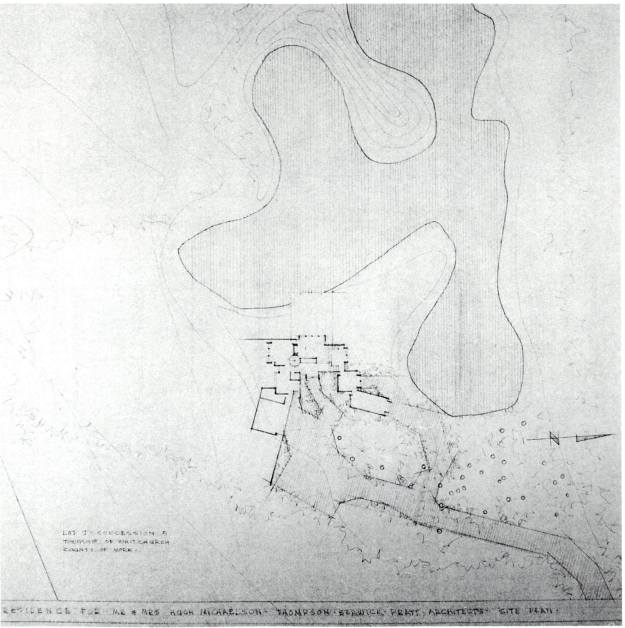

LOT 7 CONCESSION 5
TOWNSHIP OF WHITCHURCH
COUNTY OF YORK.

RESIDENCE FOR MR & MRS HUGH MICHAELSON · THOMPSON · BERWICK · PRATT · ARCHITECTS · SITE PLAN ·

116

Michaelson house

Figure 116
Thom's sketch plan drawing,
Whitechurch, 1975.

Kilgour house

Figures 117 and 118
This unpretentious but large
house (1970) has a distinct
concept and quality which I
would label as a "British
Columbia ambience." It is not
usual in Ontario to build a
house of cedar boards and this
much glass, which also has a
maximum heat-losing perimeter. Conceptually, the plan is
a series of small sheds
attached to one long corridor
and parallel overhead trellis.
This description is not meant
to denigrate the genius of the
plan and siting, including the
simplicity and variety of the
internal spaces and the views
of the surrounding private
landscape it affords. Some
sense of the constantly changing effects of transparency and
reflection with the seasonal
changes can be seen in the
photograph, although it shows
only one end of the house.
This is an unadulterated West
Coast house converted to deal
with Ontario snow (by elimi-
nating overhangs).

118

117

lines indicate
scope of
photograph,
above

In the midst of the Trent projects, Thom had started to develop the schematic design for the Donald Fraser house in Toronto. He then turned it over to Paul Merrick, who, with Brian Kilpatrick, completed it. Merrick was the Romantic Thom saw in himself, and in addition, he brought the hands-on skills of a boat builder and craftsman. Thom gave him a free hand, and the house is a remarkable demonstration of the three-dimensional free-form spatial planning and virtuosity in construction that reveal Merrick's strengths. On this project he was egged on by Ron to experiment, and the results reveal the symbiotic relationship between these two architects. The quality and mood of some of the rooms have, in their size and materiality, overtones of rooms at Massey College, a phase Merrick says "they were working themselves through."[3]

Merrick conceived this version of the house, while the drawing and detailing was done with Brian Kilpatrick, who also supervised its construction. A talented designer also, Kirkpatrick created several large light fixtures for the house that give a special quality to the interior environment. He was another of Thom's protégés whose work was inspired by him and in whom Thom had complete confidence.

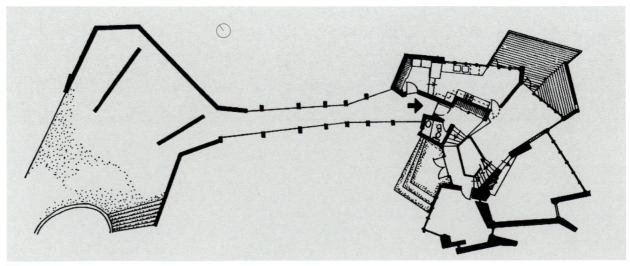

119

Fraser house

Figure 119
Plan.

Figure 120
The house as it is first seen
from the driveway approach.
The floor of the covered walkway to the front door is three
feet lower than the lawn area
above and completely open to
the ravine on the other side.

Barbara Frum, in her eulogy to Thom at his funeral, described the process she and her husband, Murray, went through as he designed their house: *Ron loved solving riddles, and we sometimes felt he built problems into his drawings so he could be summoned in desperation by anxious clients to dazzle them with the brilliance of his remedies.*[4]

Indeed, the Frum house was probably the most remarkable house Thom did in Ontario, and it was done over a period of fifteen years. What started as a commission to put a 'Big Room' on an already remodelled small house, continued almost every year with successive renovation projects for the dining room, the kitchen, the bedrooms, an exercise room, plans for a covered swimming pool (not built), and other projects including a fence, screens, the driveway paving, and so on. As Frum related:

With clients, certainly with us, there was a sense of partnership. You were needed to work the problems through with him. And the workmen, they loved him, because he knew their craft and because he loved materials so. And yet, as he resolved the endless articulation of boards and joints involved in a hand-made house, all that genius was down-played — 'that's nothin' Frum, that's just one of my tricks' . . . The Big Room he built for us remains in my mind one of the finest, most humane spaces he ever produced, an enormous, distinctively simple square, above which he slung a triangular mezzanine—both levels cantilevered off an unornamented slab of caramel brick—the whole hunkered down under a shallow hill and was married to the landscape through the mediation of suspended trellisses.

Ron produced the sketch from which the room was built after four hours of just sitting by himself looking at the problem, then drew a sketch that was perfect—perfect on completion as the first day he sketched it on his note pad—and perfect to this day.

His space is never austere, it's for human beings. And we never had a visitor who didn't smile in recognition of the bracing comfort he is enveloping you in and didn't leave saying, I'd love to live here.[5]

In addition to changing the character of the house by a series of additions and renovations, Thom, with Barbara and Murray Frum, completely altered the character of the site by changes in the plant materials. There is a distinct feeling of the West Coast landscape, particularly on the southern ravine side of the long narrow lot with its high evergreen trees. Thom also persuaded the Frums to plant large flowering trees and shrubs in critical locations close to the house for their scent and colour, to frame views and to make it impossible to see the house all at once, the same approach he learned from Neutra and Wright and used so successfully in his own work in Vancouver.

Frum house

Figure 121
The big room.

Frum house

Figure 122
Entrance from the carport.

Figure 123
This cedar light fixture is located on top of a half-wall which separates the entry stair from the big room. It is seen as one enters the big room.

123

124

Frum house
Garden around the big room

Figure 124
Patio.

Figure 125
Lower pond.

12 Changing Times

THE KNOWLEDGE AND INFORMATION revolution of the postwar period spawned new opportunities for entrepeneurship. Simultaneously, it provided widespread access to highly technical information which tended to demystify the world of building in all its aspects. By the 1970s a much wider range of building types attracted investment and initiated a major expansion of opportunities for developers. Many of these were people with a long-term association with building in partnerships between experienced investors and realty and construction corporations, providing within their own operations financial, procurement, facilities management and technical skills—everything except design. In Canada during the 1970s, there were, as well, many small players, relatively inexperienced and marginally funded, looking for new opportunities and quick profits from smaller projects, mostly in housing and small commercial buildings. While they all needed the architect, they were more likely to approach him as a sub-contractor, and select him on the basis of stiff competition against other architects, making their judgements based on partial fees for partial services, and on his willingness to accept the corporation's total control and management of the project. In this mode, the architect was expected to provide limited specialist services only.

This usually involved accepting the client's program without question, producing a design for it in compliance with planning regulations and taking it through the procedure to obtain a building permit on the developer's behalf, all for a negotiated fee. The essential difference between this and the normal architect-client relationship is the degree of decision-making control the architect holds in the process.

Because the building is an investment opportunity, the developer/owner is usually concerned with maximizing marketability—to attract tenants at the market rates, and/or profitability—to build at the least capital and operating cost. In this environment, the tendency is to build at the highest allowable density and the minimum quality required to meet the competition in the particular market-niche where a building is located. Timing is critical. The architect is thus at the beck and call of the developer, is under time pressure and is not in control. Changes may be made after he completes his portion of the work, and without consulting him, and yet his name and reputation are associated with the project. If the developer is conscientious and the architect agrees with these decisions, the process is not necessarily bad. However, the architect may find that he has served a process and project that has turned out to be quite different from the one for which he obtained a permit, and may be drawn into lawsuits for building performance failures of what turns out to be a questionable project. He is also working on only part of the process, usually for a low fee, so that he needs many more projects to keep afloat. The danger of this situation is that the architect can become identified with and totally dependent on developer clients, and thus be extremely vulnerable to the fluctuations of the market and interest rates as they affect the financial deals between the investors. Other problems such as erratic time schedules, delays, bad management, cancellations or bankruptcy are all a risk. This can suddenly expose the architect to liability because of the interactions of variables totally beyond his control. An architect who accepts a commission from a developer must understand and accept the value system operating and the risks he is taking, and then take precautions to protect himself.

Ron Thom was trained by architects who provided full services to conservative and stable clients, from concept through construction and occupancy, with appropriate fees that allowed for a reasonable profit. As a consequence of the client's respect for their professionalism, they alone would interpret the client's requirements into building form, and would select the specialist consultants and contractors to provide the required services to bring a design to reality. In doing so they were free to question the client's intentions and requirements and to propose alternatives at the concept stage, or any other stage of the project's development regarding its cultural or social relevance, its suitability, appearance, utility, constructability, equipment or furnishing. The goal was to develop an integrated quality product. Until the mid-1970s, every commission Ron Thom had received had come in on that basis, without question, and he knew no other way to work. He became extremely wary about getting involved in this new, different mode of operation, and rightly felt it would compromise his freedom as an architect, and ultimately, his work.[1]

According to Alastair Grant, "Ron didn't know why he got work other than houses, and he never had any idea of how to get work or how he got work . . . he was complex and shy . . . he pretended he couldn't believe how people would see him as being any good, but he was disappointed if they didn't know!!" Having tried many times to discuss this problem with him, Grant quotes Thom as saying, "Look . . . you hang out your shingle . . . if they want you they'll come and see you . . . I can show them what I can do, I design buildings, that's it!! . . . I can talk to them about their problem, and if I like what it is they are proposing, and I can tell them what I can do for them and if we can come to some agreement, we will proceed."[2] This statement lays out the architect's credo as he had learned it by observation. It is based on the necessity to hold himself separate and independent, laying down his own terms to maintain his absolute freedom to make his own design decisions.

Admirable as it is, Thom's partners were not as convinced as he was that the firm could count on that approach to keep the work coming in in the competitive climate of Toronto in the mid-1970s. They were up against the classic dilemma of the architect: 'how do you maintain your integrity and still put food on the table?' They were also more conscious than he that architects from a new and ambitious generation were appearing on the scene quite prepared to work in this business-oriented environment, who brought with them different values and a new aesthetic or style. Post-Modernism was rapidly catching on with the new developers in their search for novelty, and for a competitive edge in the market.

Ron Thom and the rest of our generation of architects were initiated into modernism by the architects whose work we admired because it was new to us, different from what we saw around us, and yet, connected to our environment. As Ron said, "we developed a predilection towards certain ideas about architecture rather than certain others."[3] We each had our favourite architects and buildings, and we experimented, trying to grasp the principles of plan organization, site analysis and orientation, structure and form while trying to use their formal vocabulary in our location and environment.

We never thought of what we were doing as learning a "style"—that was a word associated with the old ways of the Beaux-Arts architects and not relevant to our time. The notion that an architect could work in more than one way or style, as they did, was anathema to us. We scorned architects who attempted to respond to the new wave of modernism by tacking bits and pieces onto the same old plans (signs and symbols of the new style as they saw it) to show that they were 'with it'. These bits and pieces were quickly labelled "clichés," and taboo.

As more and more modernist buildings were built, the word "style" came up frequently as the historians, the critics and the magazines, after the fact, were able to identify and describe the elements of a clear formal language used in three or more buildings. Hitchcock and Johnson's "International style"[4] led the way. Regional features inspired the "Bay Region style," the "Northwest style," and specific buildings were said to represent "the Chicago style," and so it went.

The sudden arrival of Post-Modernism with its direct links to the wave of consumerism in the late 1970s and 80s and the blatant individualism of a suddenly affluent sector of the postwar baby-boom generation caught Thom and our generation by surprise, rendering most of us speechless, if not obsolete. Modernism and its failure, as the Post-Modernists were saying at every turn, were the main targets, particularly in the design and austerity of the single family house or apartment building, or in the box-like office buildings of the day. The attack was led by a new crop of art and architectural historians and theorists followed by prominent architects and interior designers. In a consumer-driven market Post Modernism was an instant commercial success with the developers and the design-based industries. What we have seen over the past fifteen years is some brilliant and stunning buildings, many bad imitations of them and a cliché-ridden plethora of shopping malls, condominium and office towers internationally distributed. These have been put together from a choice of thousands of wonderful new materials, products, appliances and components and new technologies, many at extravagant and unconscionable costs, indicating the global spread of 'high-end' consumerism.

Ron Thom had little time for any of this. As far as he was concerned, "architects are terrible dogmatists and decree makers. It is not enough to simply do something—but this must always be explained—preferably with some new theory, or even more preferably, one of one's own."[5]

He could rationalize every feature of his buildings in terms of its functional or technical suitability, or the logic of its form as responding to the site, the weather or a client's needs separately or collectively as a harmonious whole. He saw no reason to label what he was doing, or to change as a response to current fashion (or "vogue" as he called it).

As the reality sank in with the partners that Thom was unwilling to adapt to these new trends, and was no longer able to bring in work as before, they had to assess where they were going to put their effort.

With the completion of the Shaw Festival Theatre in 1973, Peter Smith gave up his partnership and joined Bill Lett, who had left the firm in 1967, to establish their own firm. This was a major blow for Thom so soon after the formation of his new firm. The loss of two of the original four key colleagues caused a second reorganization of the new firm, and a name change to "The Thom Partnership/Architects and Planners." There were no additions to the remaining partners (Thom, Grant and Sai-Chew) at this time. Thom's drinking and its effect on the office were clearly issues that had to be faced and further attempts were made to get him some professional help. He finally responded to the pressure and committed himself to a treatment program. This is confirmed by those close to him in the firm and in his family. It turned out to be a gesture he could not sustain, but it relieved strained relationships for a while.

According to Dick Sai-Chew, "the firm had to find a new client base, and the best opportunities lay in the development area."[6] By this he meant that it was becoming clear by the mid-1970s that the urban core of Toronto and the smaller regional centres were all on the verge of major rapid development, most of it in high-density, high-quality, office and commercial buildings and condominiums, and that all of it would be done by the larger developers. To stay in the top-ranking architectural firms in Toronto, Thom and his partners would have to learn who was whom in this particular client world, and then reorganize the firm and learn to provide the services these developers were looking for.

At this point, 1976, Alastair Grant decided that he had to leave. It was a particularly difficult decision for him as he had been there from the start of the practice in Toronto, and he had been very close to both Ron and Molly. He felt this was a turning point and the end of the office he had known and helped build. He had no confidence that Thom could adjust to what was about to happen to the firm, and he could no longer live with Thom's erratic and unpredictable behaviour.[7] For Thom, this was yet another but more devastating blow, as he had relied on Alastair for so many years.

Thom and Sai-Chew made an attempt to recover by appointing two of the next most senior staff, Brian Kilpatrick and Michael Miller, as partners. During the next four years three different events ocurred that changed the course of the firm decisively. The type of work which the new partners were interested in, which was the same as Thom's and Grant's interests, dried up, and the new partners, too, became worried about Ron's ability to keep the firm together. They left after two years. Two separate major developers approached Thom with projects which were unusual and therefore interesting, but which set a precedent for the office which Thom later regretted. In 1980, Molly decided to take the children and separate from Ron, so that he was preoccupied with the lead-up to and the aftermath of that decision, including helping her and the children to get resettled in another area of the city.

SEPARATION FROM MOLLY effectively ended any regular contact with his second family and considerably reduced his contact with many of their mutual friends in Toronto. Approaching sixty, Thom set himself up in an apartment downtown, but he was only partially able to look after himself, and his health deteriorated still further. He had become notorious for his late-night long-distance phone calls to his many friends outside Toronto, during which he would pour out his current frustrations and problems. If the response was less than what he wanted to hear he would have tantrums that further reduced those friendships. His depressions became more frequent and sent him deeper into alcoholism at a time when there were fewer friends to steer him into a safe haven to sober up and recover his self-esteem, at least enough to face the world.

There were, however, a number of single women friends in Vancouver and Toronto, most of them independent professional businesswomen near his own age, on whom he began to rely to take him in. They would come and get him if necessary, and nurse him through the worst stages, and then listen to his version of whatever it was that had started the cycle. They responded to his romantic nature, they were good listeners with no direct knowledge of his world and therefore open to his version of events, not critical of his views and in awe of his "genius." The intimacy of this confessional and the mental stroking it provided was important to the restoration of his ego and sense of himself. He would spend one or two days with them, or sometimes much longer. These visits frequently included long drives and walks in the countryside or along the coastline to restore his contact with his old haunts. He would involve himself building or doing something useful to earn his keep. The result was that he would usually be sober and refreshed when he left their company.[8]

BACK IN THE OFFICE with few job prospects and a critical situation on his hands, Thom was persuaded to investigate the two developers proposals despite his qualms about the process. Fortunately, both were for challenging and innovative projects requiring full design and production services.

The first of these projects was Atria North,[9] built in 1978 in the Toronto suburb of North York for Marathon Realty, a major developer with projects across Canada. As owners, they were aware of a potential demand for prime office space located in developing suburban centres close to upscale market housing and mass transit, to provide an alternative destination to the downtown core with its commuting problems and extreme congestion. They commissioned Thom to develop the master plan for four low-rise office buildings with a total floor area of 1.4 million square feet, set in a twenty-two-acre landscaped site. The buildings were to be four storeys in height, connected by two levels of underground parking for 3,200 cars. Each building was square in plan, with a square atrium in each, covered with a glass roof. This format offers wide floors with large windows on both sides, and a striking and peaceful view into the year-round atrium garden. The form of the building offers a very energy-efficient shell, combined with the option of open planning and excellent net/gross floor area efficiency. Unfortunately,

only the first of the four buildings was built. It appears that the alternative, a Post-Modern high-rise office tower, was more seductive to the Toronto developer's clients at that time.

The second project, Confederation Square, involved a whole city block in the heart of downtown Toronto, half of which was covered by an existing building of heritage value which the City wanted to keep. The developer was proposing that the air rights over that half of the site be transferred to the other half of the site, which could then support a major office building with an internal atrium and multi-level shopping area on the lower floors. The existing building was to be renovated, and the internal spaces integrated, wherever appropriate, with the new buildings. In addition, the exterior was to pick up the "lines" of the old building, particularly on the lower levels to further the sense of integration. The project was commissioned as a joint-venture between the Thom Partnership and the firm of Moryama and Tshima.

The first phase, getting a development permit, was carried out, but in the end, the developer was not able to persuade the City to allow the whole scheme as proposed. The developer then split the project into two separate buildings, giving the Thom office the go-ahead to renovate and restore the historical buildings, hiring the Moryama firm to design the tower based on a revised program, which, as it turned out, was not accepted either. Some time later, an envelope-filling, glass-walled, unrelated tower of monstrous proportion and no architectural merit was built on the site by a still different group. Thom had personally lost interest after the first scheme, and the experience, coupled with the letdown of the Atria project, tended to confirm his doubts about the whole development process as it had come to be practised.

Atria North office building

Figure 126
Atrium glazing detail.

Figure 127
The Atrium.

127

126

THROUGHOUT THIS PERIOD, Murray Beynon had been showing design and leadership skills in the office and some familiarity and ease with the new client world, so, in 1979 Thom and Sai-Chew invited him to become a partner, with a mandate to build a new client base for the firm. By then, there was a slowdown in development in the Toronto area, and the signs of another downturn in the market, and a federal election was imminent. One of the first decisions the new partnership took was to open an office in Calgary, which was the fastest growing city in Canada at that time.

The Calgary office was immediately active with a flurry of developer projects of varying scale. The first of these was a highly successful revised version of the Atria North project, this time for the Carma Corporation. Beynon produced that work from Toronto, commuting to Calgary. Within the first year of operation, the firm took another decision: to joint-venture with the Montreal firm ARCOP, headed by Ray Affleck. They merged their two branch offices in Calgary, and then opened another office together in Vancouver. Sai-Chew moved to Vancouver to head up that office, and Ron Thom stayed in Toronto, although he kept in close touch with these developments.

With things quietened down in Toronto, Thom received notice that he was to be made an Officer of the Order of Canada in the 1981 round of Canada's most prestigious awards. This could not have come at a better time. The presentation at Government House in Ottawa by the Governor-General did wonders for Thom's morale and restored some of his self-confidence at a crucial time in his life.

Again, external events intervened, this time in the form of the federal Liberal government's infamous 1981 budget which virtually wiped out MURBs[10] and with them, whole segments of the development industry, bankrupting in the process many architectural firms across the country. The recession it signalled deflated the boom in Calgary. Fortunately, Thom's office was not involved in speculative housing development, and was able to hang on until the end of 1982, when it had to close both western joint offices and retrench to Toronto in the hope that the economy would recover faster there. The Calgary office had been profitable for a while, but the Vancouver office had not produced as expected. Dick Sai-Chew returned to Toronto. Thom tried to sustain a Vancouver office for a while, but despite a major effort to obtain work through his network of friends and past clients, he found himself out of step there, too, with them and with the new breed of developer-clients. There was no avoiding the fact that the move had been a financial disaster, and that the firm was in serious trouble. Beynon moved quickly to get the firm involved in a series of proposals for development projects in Toronto, some of which were successful.

By this time Thom was getting more and more uncomfortable with some of the small-scale commercial work which was going out of the firm in his name, mostly because it didn't interest him, but he was increasingly ineffective when he tried to intervene. As a result he was drinking heavily and relapsing into various escape modes, even planning a return to Vancouver to live. As well, his health was giving out. He had been making some half-hearted attempts to get professional help for his drinking problem, but his resistance proved stronger than the cure.

IN 1982 THOM WAS INVITED to participate in a limited competition to select architects for the National Gallery of Canada and the National Museum of Man (which subsequently became the Canadian Museum of Civilization),[11] the largest architectural commissions to emerge from the federal government in years. He was one of five architects chosen to compete for the commission to design the National Gallery project. Seven others would compete for the National Museum of Man project. The competition was the brainchild of Dr. Jean Boggs, who had been appointed by Prime Minister Pierre Trudeau as Chair of the Canada Museum Construction Corporation to build these two projects. (A third project, the Aircraft Museum, was authorized at the same time to be designed and built by Public Works Canada simultaneously.) The competition was unusual in format, and in the invitation to the competitors Boggs said: "any sketches should be a measure of your imagination." What the corporation was after was conceptual ideas for how to develop these projects on specific sites. The competition period was just over a month. The selection of the competitors was in itself an unusual process during which Boggs travelled from coast to coast and made an extraordinary effort to locate and visit eighty firms, including new young architects as well as established offices.

THOM WAS JUBILANT and excited. He had interpreted Boggs's visit to his office and the news that he was in a group of only five competitors as an indication that he had an inside track. The group included him, Arthur Erickson, Barton Myers, Peter Rose and Guy Jerin-Lajoie. He saw this invitation as the means to confirm his credibility. Unfortunately, he was in no condition to be able to roll up his sleeves and lead the team. Beynon, with Steve Quigley, took over the project, and, consulting with Thom as much as possible, developed a credible scheme within the deadline. Thom was deeply disappointed when the firm's submission did not win the commission, and outraged when Moshe Safdie,

Excerpt from Jean Boggs's *Introduction* to a Special Supplement edition of *Section A* magazine, August 1984, devoted to presenting the twelve proposals for the two Museums resulting from this limited competition:

When the Canada Museums Corporation was established in February 1982, it was given a fixed amount of money, $186,600,000, and five years within which to build two large buildings for the National Gallery of Canada and the National Museum of Man. Since time and money were limited, an architectural competition was never seriously considered, especially given the fact that two competitions had already been held for the Gallery, one in 1952 and one in 1976, without leading to the construction of the winning entries.

It was decided that these two prestigious cultural institutions had to be designed by Canadians. The officers of the Corporation therefore visited some eighty architectural firms throughout the country and finally selected five of them to submit proposals for the National Gallery of Canada, and seven for the National Museum of Man.

In the letter written to each of the twelve architects on 10 December 1982, I asked them to put aside three weeks for the proposals and to have them in our offices by 17 January 1983. I added, "The proposals should be in writing but could include illustrations; nothing should exceed 8-1/2 x 11 inches. As one of our Board members puts it, "any sketches should be a measure of your imagination and not a design for the National Museum of Man (or the National gallery)." I asked that the architects address issues such as the context in which the Museum (or Gallery) would be placed, emphasize the role of the institution, and suggest an approach to an architectural solution including ways to deal with a major interior space. I made it clear that staff members from the corporation and from the museums would be ready for interviews in this period.

The letter concluded, "Although we are asking for proposals from you for one museum, this does not preclude your still being considered for the other." In fact, this did happen. Moshe Safdie, who submitted a proposal for the Museum of Man, was asked to design the National Gallery.

who had participated in the competition for the Canadian Museum of Man project, was awarded the commission for the National Gallery. His outrage is hard to understand considering the clause in Boggs's letter of invitation which stated: "Although we are asking for proposals from you for one museum, this does not preclude your being considered for the other," which gave the sponsors the right to mix and match as they saw fit.

THOM'S CONDITION BY THIS TIME was widely known.[12] While his reputation as a designer still attracted work to the office, it was also becoming clear that Beynon was providing the administrative leadership and de facto guarantee of successful production and completion of projects in that office. During 1983, Beynon raised the issue of his status in the partnership, asking for a restructuring and other conditions as well as a name change reflecting his major participation. Thom was supportive, but he could not agree to the name change, and so they were never able to reach a decision. For him, it was a matter of principle: the firm name stated what he still believed, that he was the principal owner, that he was in charge, and that the firm was committed to his clients. That belief was the basis of his pride and self-esteem. To accept a change in the firm name was to announce that he was no longer in control, and, despite the evidence that this was the case in operational terms, he was not prepared to do that. After more than a year spent trying to resolve their differences, Beynon left the firm in the fall of 1984.

The successive resignations of partners, with no new work coming in because of the sluggish economy, in addition to the continuing cost of operation and of carrying their liability, left Thom and Sai-Chew with a major financial crisis. This could only be resolved by the immediate infusion of new money which neither of them could raise under these circumstances.

The liability problem arises from architects' responsibility for the performance of their buildings over time, as it continues after completion and turnover to the client. Hence liability accumulates with the number of projects completed. Many architects carry liability insurance to cover the eventuality of litigation, to recover costs arising from a building failure, and to protect their reputation. The amount is usually based on their estimate of the probability and costs of a lawsuit at any given time. Thus "carrying the liability" is a major item in the calculation of the bottom line of the operating budget required to prevent bankruptcy.

When a firm gets into difficulty, the situation can never be kept entirely secret, particularly in a small office, and this one was no exception. By the fall of 1985, bankruptcy was in the balance for the Thom office, dependent on the successful completion of one major project, a large shopping centre, which, after a hiatus, had come alive and was under development. Stephen Quigley, who had been with the firm for several years, was leading the project.

Thom and Sai-Chew agreed to open discussions with Quigley and two others in the firm, Peter Berton and Paul Nevins, offering to consider restructuring the partnership and to discuss ways and means to save the firm. Because of Thom's age and health, the issue of the extent and nature of his participation in a revised partnership became the central obstacle to a solution. The discussions that started with good intentions and alternative proposals became more and more acrimonious. Thom insisted on retaining his position of control, and the new candidates would not agree to come in unless he stepped aside to some associate relationship. With this obstacle unresolved, the bank intervened, bringing matters to a head. Unable to produce an alternative, Thom had to agree to relinquish his control, and accept the terms offered. Under the name, "The Thom Partnership, Architects and Planners," the partnership was restructured, passing control to Sai-Chew and the three new partners. Thom's participation was redefined and his reputation saved, and the financial issues were resolved.

Thom did not accept this situation gracefully. For him this was a direct insult, a loss of 'face' offending his sense of loyalty and affecting his responsibility to his clients. He could not get used to his situation. He felt as if he had been "blackmailed" and "banished to a basement office." He was confused and frustrated, which led him to display his outrage, both in and out of the office. After a year of this, by September 1986 his retaliation was so disruptive and potentially damaging that the partners had to put him on leave for six months on the condition that he stay away from the office during that period, and in the hope that he would find a way to accept what had happened. For him, this move was the "coup de grâce." He was shattered, isolated from his life's work.

Sometime later he had an outstanding commitment to come to Vancouver to give a lecture at the School of Architecture at UBC, and to go on a bus tour of a number of his houses. He arrived frail but sober. His lecture was a slide show of his selection of his favourite houses, and major projects including Sir Sanford Fleming College, Atria North, Massey College, Trent University and Pearson College of the Pacific. His talk was direct, economical, clear and to the point about the essential problem in each of these buildings, and the basis of his solution. The tour was nostalgic, warm and friendly. He spent a week or two visiting friends in Vancouver, talking about his situation and presumably sounding out what he might do next. He went

to Hornby Island to see Chris and his grown-up children there, visiting each of them with their families separately, and saying good-bye to each in turn. He took his leave, setting out by car and ferry to Vancouver, where he visited with friends again for a day or two. Drinking again, he took the late flight to Toronto, arriving early in the morning. He was met by another friend who, after driving him around Toronto and environs as he sobered up from the plane trip, dropped him off that evening at his request at his apartment. Thirty-six hours later he was found dead, locked in his old office at his desk, at 7 a.m., Thursday, October 30, 1986.

Reflections

IT IS NO EXAGGERATION to say that Ron Thom, at his death, was loved and admired by a host of people with whom he had crossed paths—for his great talent, his sympathetic ear, and his engaging personality. But many also knew that there was an adverse side: his quick temper, his dependency on alcohol. For his families of two marriages, or for those of his friends and colleagues who looked after him or who experienced or bore the brunt of the dark side of his escapades repeatedly, in many cases, his behaviour finally put unacceptable strains on close personal and professional relationships. His unpredictability increasingly affected his practise, necessarily limiting his involvement and hence his effectiveness and development as an architect in the final years of his life.

For those of us who knew and admired his talent, creativity, and his architectural sensibility, the tragedy of those last years and his early death is that he was not able to realize his full potential as an architect/designer. He and his early work in Vancouver had made a strong and positive impression on a wide diversity of clients and friends through the 1950s and the early 1960s. From the age of forty, the next twenty-three years of his career were developed in the highly competitive environment of Toronto through a period of major expansion, with remarkable success. Two major projects, Massey College and Trent University, established his reputation and presence, bringing him international recognition and awards as well as a steady stream of substantial but smaller projects which he carried out with distinction. Additionally, he had become widely recognized in Toronto for his service to the arts community.

However, by the mid-1970s his fortunes had started to change significantly as external forces changed the business side of architecture in ways Thom was ill-equipped to deal with, and his practise declined. It is also clear that there was very little growth and development of *his* architectural ideas to be seen in the work of his practise in those last ten years, and no evidence of moves on his part to develop an organizational response to the new practise environment, or, when his colleagues attempted to break into that world, to encourage them. One explanation of his lack of response in this situation was his inability to concentrate during the latter part of that period, most likely attributable to alcohol abuse and failing health, together with the increasing uncertainty concerning his future, his fear that the firm might fail, and his tendency to escape from his problems rather than confront them. When others finally confronted him with the loss of control of his firm, in his terms 'the ultimate humiliation', he fought them tooth and nail. He was unsuccessful, but the result was inevitable, under the circumstances.

Despite the important work Thom accomplished in eastern Canada he continues to be identified by his peers as a West Coast architect. His profound feeling for nature—its changing climate and moods, its many configurations and forms—nurtured as a child growing up in Vancouver, where the presence of nature is pervasive, and developed as a young man of unusual sensibilities—is reflected in all that he did. It is reflected in his design, his writing and thinking, and gives character to the particular place he has won for himself in the development of modernist architecture in Canada.

Figure 128
Ron Thom, 1983 portrait.

Notes

Chapter 2: Growing Up

1 Minutes of meetings of the Estevan Methodist Sunday School indicate that Elena Fennell was appointed there as a teacher on July 1, 1913, as organist on April 29 the same year, and resigned on January 2, 1914. Copies of those Minutes were made available by the Estevan Public library.

2 The information in this paragraph was provided by a letter from Iain Mentiplay, Q.C., Secretary-Treasurer, The Law Society of Saskatchewan, ref. file B-694, August 8, 1991.

3 The quoted paragraph appears in Lynn McDonald, M.P., *The Party That Changed Canada* (Toronto: Macmillan of Canada, 1987), p. 8. A chapter end note in that book indicates that the reference for this paragraph is a quotation from Richard Allen, *The Social Passion* (Toronto: The University of Toronto Press, 1973), p. 73f.

4 Dates confirmed by letter from the Personnel Records Centre, Department of Veterans Affairs, National Archives of Canada, December 16, 1991.

5 Thom's "Education Progress Record" in Elementary, Junior High and High School, and the Vancouver School of Art is now held by Robert McMillan, Registrar, the Emily Carr College of Art, Vancouver, who provided me with a copy for reference.

6 A copy of Thom's "Record of Service in the Royal Canadian Air Force" was provided by the Personnel Records Centre, Department of Veterans Affairs of Canada, Ottawa.

Chapter 3: Finding a Focus

1 The source of career information on B.C. Binning used in this chapter was the catalogue for a retrospective exhibition of his work at the Fine Arts Gallery, University of British Columbia, March 13 through 31, 1973.

2 Scott Watson, "Art in Living," *Vancouver Art and Artists, 1931-1983* (Vancouver: Vancouver Art Gallery, 1983), p. 75.

3 Ron Thom, notes for a talk he gave on March 4, 1986, for the "B.C. Binning Exhibition," at the McMichael Canadian Collection, Kleinburg, Ontario, May 4, 1986, from a collection of his papers held by Molly Thom, copied by the author with permission.

4 This information on the cost of lots and taxes was obtained by me in 1948 from Ron as I was going to buy one there myself.

Chapter 4: The Firm

1 Lists and drawings of many of these early Sharp and Thompson houses can be seen at the University of Calgary Architectural Archive. Many of the houses are in the Shaughnessy area, the most mature and wealthy subdivision in Central Vancouver, developed by the Canadian Pacific Railway.

2 These figures are as remembered by my colleagues. There is perhaps some exaggeration, but they are not far off.

3 Excerpt from notes of an interview with Ned Pratt, February 16, 1991.

4 Excerpt from article, "Thompson, Berwick, and Pratt," *Canadian Architect,* June 1961, vol. 6, p. 55.

Chapter 5: Apprenticeship

1 Excerpt from notes of an interview with Molly Bobak, February 27, 1992.

2 Richard Neutra, *Survival through Design* (New York: Oxford University Press, 1954). This book was one of the first books directed to architects that started to probe the results of new research in the sciences on the long-term physical effects of buildings on their occupants, showing Neutra's newly built solutions that were supposed to solve these problems. They greatly influenced the awareness of young architects of the day and gave inspiration and impetus to some of the early experiments in environmentally responsive buildings in the 1960s.

3 Excerpt from exhibition catalogue, Arthur Drexler/ Thomas S. Hines, *The Architecture of Richard Neutra: From Internationl Style to California Modern* (New York, The Museum of Modern Art, 1982), p. 54.

4 Excerpts from eulogy written for Ron Thom's funeral by Barbara Frum, November 1986, unpublished, used here with her permission.

5 Excerpt from notes of conversation with Bob Gibson, who was one of the participants.

6 The term "Usonian" was used by Frank Lloyd Wright to identify a series of houses he developed based on a modular grid planning system and a set of standard details.

7 The reference to the book, *The Mysteries and Reality of the Site*, attributed to Richard Neutra, comes from my memory, and I have not been able to verify that the book really existed in the forties and fifties.

8 Excerpt from notes of an interview with Ned Pratt, February 16, 1991.

9 Excerpt from notes of an interview with John Wallace, January 26, 1991.

10 From a conversation with Michael Miller, May 27, 1993.

Chapter 6: Becoming an Architect

1 From a conversation with Ned Pratt, June 1994.

2 Excerpts from notes of an interview with Dave Hickman, February 28, 1992.

3 Ned Pratt attributes Dr. Tom Howarth, Dean of the University of Toronto School of Architecture, with the suggestion to use Italian mosaic tile for the BC Electric tower. Howarth visited Vancouver briefly just after his return from Italy and a tour of a factory there.

4 Excerpts from notes of an interview with Dave Hickman, February 28, 1992.

5 Excerpts from notes of an interview with Ned Pratt, April 26, 1991.

6 Excerpts from notes of an interview with John Wallace, January, 1991.

7 Excerpts from notes of an interview with Ned Pratt, April 26, 1991.

Chapter 7: Houses West

1 Excerpted from "Ron Thom Houses in Vancouver," *Canadian Architect*, vol. 17, March 1962, pp. 39-47.

This article has plans and excellent photographs of seven of the best of Thom's Vancouver houses.

Chapter 8: Massey College

1 The background for the second and third paragraphs was provided by a letter from Vincent Massey dated January 17, 1929 to Burgon Bickersteth, who later became the Warden of Hart House, available in the Massey Archives, Graduate Library, the University of Toronto, box A75-0021-048. The letter is in answer to various enquiries from the Warden as to the antecedents of Hart House and provides an interesting insight into the importance of that project to the university in the 1920s, as well as the depth of Vincent Massey's contribution to that project, and his programmatic and architectural sensibility. Excerpts are reproduced here by permission of the Massey Foundation and the Master of Massey College.

2 Claude Bissell, *The Young Vincent Massey* (Toronto: University of Toronto Press, 1981), p. 62.

3 Vincent Massey, *What's Past Is Prologue* (New York: St. Martin's Press, 1964), pp. 527-28. Excerpts reproduced with the permission of the Massey Foundation.

4 Claude Bissell, *The Imperial Canadian* (Toronto: University of Toronto Press, 1983), p. 296.

5 Vincent Massey, *What's Past is Prologue*, p. 528.

6 In a limited competition of this type, the sponsor is completely in charge of the selection, instruction and remuneration of the participants and is also the judge and jury.

7 By permission of the Massey Foundation, copies of relevant correspondence, including the letter of invitation and the memorandum sent to the participants, were made from the private files of the Massey Foundation, and provided by the National Archive, Canada, in Ottawa. These include details of the Competition correspondence, as well as those in notes 10-15 following,

8 Vincent Massey, *What's Past is Prologue*, p. 529.

9 Claude Bissell, *The Imperial Canadian*, p. 298.

10 Excerpt from letter to John Parkin, July 4, 1960, from Vol. 6, File 3, Massey Foundation Files, National

Archives, Canada, Ottawa.

11 Excerpt from Carmen Corneil's report accompanying his Round 1 submission, from Vol. 6, File 3, MF Files, National Archives, Canada, Ottawa, p. 2.

12 Excerpt from Trustees' written comments re Thom's Round 1 submission, Vol. 6, File 3, MF Files, National Archives, Canada, Ottawa.

13 The critique for the three ongoing competitors, together with the letters of invitation to continue in Round two are from Vol. 6, File 3, MF Files, National Archives, Canada, Ottawa.

14 Excerpt from Carmen Corneil's Report accompanying his Round 1 submission, Vol. 6, File 3, MF Files, National Archives Canada, Ottawa, p. 3.

15 The reference is to a letter from Corneil to Massey, Vol. 6, File 3, MF Files, National Archives Canada, Ottawa.

16 *Canadian Architect*, December 1960,Vol. 5, No. 12, p. 41.

17 Thompson, Berwick, Pratt, Architects, Vancouver, working drawings for Massey College, and shop drawings by Ritchie Stone Company, dated October 16, 1961, by permission of the Master and Marie Corey, Librarian and Archivist, Massey College.

18 The leather sling chairs in the Great Hall dining area are the cause of this jibe. It is my opinion and that of one or two others, at least, who are of the same size and bulk and also have lower back problems as I have.

19 Claude Bissell, *The Imperial Canadian*, pp. 295-96.

20 Claude Bissell, *The Imperial Canadian*, p. 297.

21 Comment by Senior Fellow, Massey College, who prefers to remain anonymous, in a dining room conversation, June 1993.

22 Excerpt from Peter Collins, critique in "The Arts," *Manchester Guardian*, November 28, 1963.

23 From notes of a discussion with Arthur Erickson in Vancouver, September 25, 1991.

24 Article by Brigitte Shim, "Art and Function," *The Massey Bull, 1963-93, Special Anniverary Edition*, an in-house limited publication printed by the Massey College Press, summer, 1993. By permission of the author, the Master and a fellow of Massey College.

Chapter 9: Trent University

1 A.O.C. Cole, *Trent: The Making of a University: 1957-87* (Peterborough: Trent University, 1993), p. 9.

2, 3 and 4 From notes of an interview with Denis Smith, October 16-17, 1991, and from copies of reports and other papers from his files of committee meetings, etc., provided as background information to our discussion, excerpted here with his permission.

5 Quotation from T.H.B. Symons's address at the opening ceremonies of Trent University, published in a commemorative book recording the event, *Opening Ceremonies—Trent University*, October 1964, p. 16.

6 From notes of an interview with the T.H.B. Symons, October 16, 1991.

7 The information about the procedure for the choice of architect was provided by Denis Smith in an interview, October 17, 1991.

8 The very important background regarding the surprisingly unenthusiastic reaction of the Vancouver office to Thom's winning the commission was discussed with me by John Dayton, a partner in TBP, in an interview, January 29, 1991. It is most relevant to Chapter 10 regarding details leading up to the severance of the TBP and Thom partnership in 1970.

9 From notes of an interview with Bob McIntyre, June 6, 1991.

10 A.O.C. Cole, *Trent: The Making of a University*, p. 22.

11 From notes of an interview with Denis Smith, October 16-17, 1991.

12 On his return, Thom made several reports to the parent committees regarding the two trips, *Report of the Planning Architect—Abroad Thoughts From Home*, July 1963, and a second one on the New England excursion. They are both excellent observations. Copies were provided by Trent University Archives and excerpted with permission

13 The quotation is excerpted from the brief to the architect by the campus planning committee at the start of the design of Champlain College. It appeared in a

major article, "Trent University," *Canadian Interiors,* June 1991, as part of a segment by Ron Thom entitled "Architect's Statement," pp. 30-31.

14 See A.O.C. Cole, *Trent: The Making of a University,* pp. 35-37 for background to the decision to make Trent an all-electric campus.

15 Excerpt from Ron Thom, *Report to Board of Governors on the Master Plan,* Trent University, courtesy of the Trent University Archive.

16 As told to me by Ron Thom in 1964, the day after he drew it.

17 Diagram from "Trent University: Architecture for a Special Curriculum," *Architecural Record,* September 1969, p. 152, an excellent and thorough photo coverage and thoughtful commentary on the campus in its early days.

18 For a complete description of this work see Morden Yolles, "Engineer," *Canadian Architect,* December 1967, p. 32.

19 From an interview with T.H.B. Symons, October 19, 1991.

20 These would include *Canadian Architect, Architecture Canada, Architectural Record* (U.S.), *Canadian Interiors,* plus a feature chapter in Carol Moore-Ede, *Canadian Architecture, 1960/70* (Toronto: Burns and MacEachern, 1968), p. 46. Another feature article appears in Leon Whiteson, *Modern Canadian Architecture* (Edmonton: Hurtig Publishers, 1983), p. 128.

21 From a critique by Arthur Erickson, "Trent University," *Canadian Interiors,* June 1969, p.29.

22 The material in the following paragraphs was put together from notes of conversations with some of the major actors involved with the first phase of the development of Trent University, as well as faculty and student users, architects and other critics on and off campus in order to form an overview of how successful Thom's concept as realized has been, and what lies ahead.

23 Excerpt from conference paper, edited and reprinted in "Voice," *The Canadian Architect,* July 1970. The event was the The International College and University Conference Exposition, meeting in Atlantic City, at which Thom won four of seven awards in architecture presented for four of his buildings at Trent University. He was singled out for these awards from 140 entrants in the competition.

Chapter 10: Transition

1 "Megastructure" is a word attributed to Reyner Banham, a British architectural historian, to describe an emerging building prototype, the very large multi-functional building, typically large enough to house a whole town-centre.

2 Excerpted from notes of an interview with Bob Murtrie, May 25, 1993.

3 Excerpted from notes of an interview with Otto Safir, January 29, 1991, a structural engineer and partner in TBP from February 1964.

4 Excerpted from notes of an interview with John Wallace, January 26, 1991, an Associate who was required to attend the Board meetings.

5 Excerpted from notes of an interview with Ned Pratt, December 12, 1991.

6 Ibid.

7 Detailed background information for this and preceding paragraphs was provided from notes of interviews with all the persons involved and named here, and from detailed correspondence and personal records kept by George Giles in his capacity as Chief Architect for the government client and this project. With his permission and collaboration, the latter documents allowed us to reconstruct the sequence of events in considerable detail. The paragraphs referred to provide a minimal account of those events relevant to this book.

8 Excerpted from a collection of notes for and drafts of articles and talks hand-written by Ron Thom, held by Molly Thom and reviewed with her permission.

Chapter 11: Houses East

1 Excerpts from a collection of notes for and drafts of articles and talks hand-written by Ron Thom, held by Molly Thom and quoted here with her permission.

2 In the 1960s, the University of Calgary in Calgary, Alberta, created the Canadian Architectural Archives and launched an aggressive collection program to obtain the complete drawing and building records of the major postwar architects across Canada, a program that was, initially, highly successful. The files of Sharp, Thompson, Berwick, Pratt and all of its successive incarnations are there and include many of the projects on which Ron Thom worked. Unfortunately, these include only a small number of his house projects because so many of them were done on overtime, before more formal documentary procedures were introduced by the firm, and have disappeared. His Toronto work, done originally in the name of the Vancouver firm, went to the same archive, and when he opened his own office he continued the practice of sending all of the files to Calgary. Again, however, as much of the housework was done informally, as described in this book, many of the individual project files are far from complete (no fault of the archivists). The numbers of houses referred to in this paragraph were calculated from the consecutively numbered and dated project lists maintained by the Toronto office as the basis for their accounting records.

3 Excerpt from notes of a conversation with Paul Merrick in December 1991.

4 and 5 Excerpts from the eulogy delivered by Barbara Frum at Thom's funeral in November 1986, quoted here with her permission.

Chapter 12: Changing Times

1 The description of the changes in the nature of practise in these pages is based on my own observations over many years, and discussions with many architects experiencing and experimenting with this form of practise. My long association with the professional organizations has verified the problems outlined and their effect on different individual architects and practises, and the pros and cons of these arrangements.

2 The quotations are from notes of an interview with Alastair Grant, October 6, 1991.

3 Excerpt from undated notes for a lecture, from a collection of unpublished papers by Ron Thom held by Molly Thom and used here with her permission.

4 Henry-Russell Hitchcock and Philip Johnson, *The International Style* (New York and London: W.W. Norton, 1966 edition, with a new Foreword and Appendix by Hitchcock).

5 Quotation excerpted from an untitled handwritten note in a collection of unpublished papers by Ron Thom, held by Molly Thom and and used here with her permission.

6 Quotation from notes of an interview with Dick Sai-Chew, August, 1991.

7 The information in this paragraph is from notes of an interview with Alastair Grant, October 6, 1991.

8 This paragraph is compiled from my own experience with Thom, and lengthy conversations with his colleagues and friends directly involved in the events discussed.

9 The details of the Atria North project were obtained from a brochure prepared by the Thom office in 1981 to make the facts available for publication, and useable for promotion.

10 The source of this phenomenon was the sudden withdrawal by the federal government of the very popular tax shelter offered as MURBs (the acronym for 'multiple unit residential buildings')—a program devised by the Liberal government to draw the investment funds of the rapidly increasing professional community (doctors, dentists, engineers, etc.) into financing the new housing requirements of their generation at high density in and around the larger cities. The program was very successful, so that its sudden withdrawal in the recession of 1981, with no notice, caught a high percentage of the less-experienced high-flyers unawares. Their failures took many building developers with them and left many contractors and architects unpaid.

11 From *Twelve Proposals for the National Gallery of Canada and for the National Museum of Man, Section A,* magazine Special Supplement, August 1984, quoted by permission of Odile Henault, editor and owner. This

edition with an Introduction by Jean Boggs, Chair of the Canada Museums Construction Corporation, is devoted to a presentation of the plans and drawings of these proposals.

13 The remaining pages of this chapter were compiled partly from memory of a conversation with Ron Thom in Vancouver in 1986, just after these events had transpired and shortly before his death. These were supplemented from my notes of meetings held in 1993-94 with the people named and others in Toronto to learn further versions and details of the events described and to construct the account in this book.

Acknowledgements

THE FOLLOWING PERSONS have contributed to this book in various ways, through conversation and interviews, direct assistance, providing ideas and crits, access to information, opening their houses, and so on. I am indebted to all of them.

Dr. and Mrs. Clifford Ames, John Andrews, Dick Archambault, Joost Baaker, Mr. and Mrs. Archie Baker, Mr. and Mrs Wilson Baker, George Baird, Essy Baniassad, Narina Bene, Murray Beynon, Jessie Binning, Doreen Boal, Molly Bobak, Richard Bolus, Bruce and Joan Boyd, Paul Buitenhuis, Bob Burniston, Peter Burton, Dennis and Adele Case, Michael Chandler, Mr. and Mrs. Ted Cohen, Dr. and Mrs. Harold Copp, Stephen Dantzer, Pat Darling, John Dayton, Jack Diamond, Dr. Morton and Mrs. Irene Dodek, Barry Downs, Macy DuBois, Roger DuToit, Mrs. Joan Dumaresq, Carol Moore Ede, Arthur Erickson, Dr. Donald Fraser, Jane Frazee, Adele Freedman, Barbara and Murray Frum, Dr. and Mrs. Gelfant, Bob Gibson, George Giles, Doug Gillmor, Mr. and Mrs. J.L. Grieg, Andrew Gruft, Alastair Grant, H. Daphne Harris, Mr. and Mrs. B.J. Hawes, Brian Hemingway, Odile Henault, Richard Henriquez, David Hickman, Fred Hollingsworth, George Hume, Dorothy Irwin, Don and Gladys Jarvis, Mr. and Mrs. Joseph Jarvis, Roy Jessiman, William Kilbourne, Brian Kilpatrick, Zoltan Kiss, Rudy Kovach, Bronwyn Ledger, Bill Lett, Linda Lewis, Blair Macdonald, Dick Mann, Geoff Massey, Hart Massey, Jack and Angus Matthews, Margaret Mayhew, James McAdam, Bill and Carole McConnell, Bob McIntyre, Dr. W.B. McLintock, Michael McMordie, Kerry McPhederan, Mr. and Mrs. Skipio Merler, Paul Merrick, Hugh Michaelson, Michael Miller, George Miller, Mr. and Mrs. Wallace Moult, Jim Murray, Bob Murtrie, Mrs. Alvin Narod, James Neufield, Paul Nevin, Peter Oberlander, R.O. Odlum, John Patkau, Mary and Gordon Payne, Bob Phillips, Joe Pincus, Donovan Pinker, Steve Quigley, Abe Rogatnick, Anne Saddlemeyer, Otto Safir, Mr. and Mrs. Hugh Segal, Denis and Dawn Smith, Gordon and Marian Smith, Peter Smith, Mr. and Mrs. Jack Southworth, Ouita Stewart, John Stubbs, Howard Sutcliffe, T.H.B. Symons, J.E. Termuende, Aaron and Margo Thom, Adam Thom, Bronwyn (Thom) Mcleod, Chris Thom, Emma Thom, Mavis Thom, Robin and Elizabeth Thom, Sydney Thom, Charles Tiers, Vincent Tovell, Hedi Trier-Pevecz, Sandy and Blanche Van Ginkel, Elanor Wachtel, Evan Walker, Ron Walkey, John Wallace, Scott Watson, Alan Wilson, Bud Wood, Morden Yolles, Kathy Zimon.

Credits

Photographs and Illustrations

The first-named person or agency supplied the original photograph or other illustration. The numbers following the names are the figure numbers (not page numbers) used to identify the illustrations in this book. The initials JF stand for John Flanders, photographer.

United Church of Canada, Victoria University Archives, Toronto, copy by JF: 1

Mavis Thom, from family collection, copy by JF: 2

Don Jarvis, copies by JF: 3-5.

John Flanders: 6, 8, 10-15, 17-24, 26, 28-32, 34-46, 48, 80-81, 83-93, 97-111, 121-27

Barry Downs: 7

Douglas Shadbolt: 9, 16, 33, 47, 74-77

TBP Collection, University of Calgary Architectural Archive, all copies by JF: 25, 27, 78-79, 94, 113-17

Massey College Library Archives, photographs and drawings reproduced with permission of the Master and Fellows of Massey College: R.J. Thom 54-57, 61-62, and Barry Downs, copies by JF: 63-65

Peter Varley: 49, 66-71, copies by University of Toronto

The Canadian Architect, December 1960, by permission, copies by JF: 50-53, 58-60

Howard Colvin and J. S. G. Simmons, *All Souls, An Oxford College and its Buildings* (Toronto:Oxford University Press, 1989), by permission: 72

Source unknown, copy by JF: 73

Richard Henriquez and Danica Djurkovic, copy by JF: 82

Paul Merrick, copies by JF: 95-96

Molly Thom, photographer unknown, copy by JF: 112

Stephen Evans, by permission of Adele Freedman, *Globe and Mail:* 118

Carol Moore Ede: 119-120

Alexander Waterhouse-Hayward: 128

Index